CROCHET FOR BEGINNERS

A Detailed Stitch Handbook to Learn and Craft Crocheting Patterns with Illustrations, Pictures and 12 Easy-to-Complete Projects

By

LETA MURPHY

© COPYRIGHT 2024 BY LETA MURPHY - ALL RIGHTS RESERVED.

Parts of this publication may not be saved in a retrieval system, copied, or transferred in any way—digitally, by scanning, recording, printing, mechanically, or in any other form—without the Publisher's written permission. Only Sections 107 and 108 of the United States Copyright Act of 1976 outline the exceptions. The publisher's publication department should be consulted about any permission concerns.

LEGAL NOTICE

The copyrights to this book are protected and can only be used for personal purposes. You cannot paraphrase, sell, copy, distribute, quote, or change any part of this book's contents without permission from the author or publisher.

DISCLAIMER NOTICE

This book has been independently written and published. Kindly note that the content contained within this publication is provided exclusively for informational and entertainment purposes. Every effort has been made to provide accurate, current, reliable, and complete information. No express or implied assurances are present. The content of this book is intended to aid readers in attaining a more comprehensive understanding of the related subject. The exercises, information, and activities are designed exclusively for self-help. This book does not intend to serve as a substitute for the counsel of professional psychologists, attorneys, financiers, or other experts. Kindly contact a certified professional if you need counseling.

Reading this work, the reader agrees that the author shall not be responsible for any direct or indirect harm caused by the content contained herein, including but not restricted to omissions, errors, or inaccuracies. You are responsible for the decisions, actions, and outcomes that ensue as a reader.

Practice makes a man perfect.
(Only if he tries hard enough)

Table of Contents

Introduction 6

Chapter 1: Yarn Craft Basics 8
1.1 Essential Tools and Equipment 10
Crochet Hooks 10
Yarn 12
Yarn Needle 13
Scissors 14
Stitch Markers 14
Measuring Tape 15
1.2 Choosing the Right Yarn and Hooks 16
Choosing Yarn 16
Holding the Yarn 20
Choosing Hooks 21
Holding Techniques for Hooks 24
1.3 Understanding Crochet Patterns 26
Deciphering Abbreviations 26
Reading Chart Patterns 32

Chapter 2: Basic Stitches 34
2.1 The Slip Knot 36
2.2 The Chain Stitch 38
2.3 The Single Crochet Stitch 40
2.4 The Double Crochet Stitch 43
2.5 The Half Double Crochet Stitch 46
2.6 The Treble Crochet Stitch 49

2.7 Double Treble Crochet.. 51
2.8 The Slip Stitch... 53

Chapter 3: Building Skills and Techniques............ 56
3.1 Adjusting Stitches in the Foundation Chain.. 58
3.2 Increasing and Decreasing Stitches.................. 59
To Increase Stitches.. 59
To Decrease Stitches.. 60
3.3 Changing Yarn Colors... 62
3.4 Weaving the Ends... 64
3.5 Making Gauge Swatch.. 65
3.6 Using Blocking Technique....................................... 66
Board Blocking... 66
Water Plunging and Towel Dry..................................... 66
Steam Iron... 67

Chapter 4: 12 Easy Crochet Projects..................... 68
4.1 Granny Square... 70
4.2 Dishcloth.. 75
4.3 Easy Scarf... 77
4.4 Beanie... 80
4.5 Simple Baby Blanket... 88
4.6 Hot Pad.. 90
4.7 Pillow Cover... 93
4.8 Laptop Case... 99
4.9 Yarn Booties for Kids.. 102
4.10 Small-Sized Amigurumi Cat................................. 105
4.11 Summer Top.. 109
4.12 Loose Cardigan.. 113

Conclusion.. 117

About the Author... 118

INTRODUCTION

Crafting starts with the love of making something with your hands. It transforms ordinary threads into valuable masterpieces through a gentle dance of fingers and a symphony of thoughts, weaving tales of creativity and imagination.

Although yarn crafts have many types such as knitting, weaving etc. other than crochet, they all cater to different needs. In crochet, the needlework techniques are different from the rest. With just one hook, it can make circles and squares with ease. The thicker the yarn size, the warmer the piece will be. You can use corresponding hooks for the kind of yarn you use to make the pieces with most ease.

I have met many people who are talented and can crochet very well from the start but stay reluctant to try at first. If only everyone could see their potential beforehand, they would be jumping at the chance to find their interest, but alas! Things don't happen just like that. You have to reach the goal by actually trying to get it.

Just look at my own story. My grandmother was a master of knitting and crocheting. When I started sewing at 14, she was my inspiration and courage behind it. She taught me with patience and gave me the confidence to become what I am today.

Everything I have accomplished to this date has resulted from her unwavering trust in my skills that I couldn't see myself at the time. Today, my reason for writing the book is the same: letting this beautiful craft live on.

If you are looking for a book that teaches you about the right tools, basic stitches, patterns, tips, and techniques, as well as provides you with several instructions to do some easy projects, you are at the right place! "Crochet for Beginners" will help you make sense of the confusing starting points of crochet that make you scratch your head or get frustrated with the whole process.

Get ready to dive into the world of crafts by forming a clear understanding of how things work, such as holding a hook, selecting the perfect yarn, and making easy and fun patterns that were too puzzling for you before by getting on to read the entire thing.

See you on the other side!

CHAPTER 1

Yarn Craft Basics

Before starting with the practicing material, let us look at the basics that you must be familiar with in order to work on crochet. It is a highly disciplined skill that requires your undivided attention for the best results.

If you are interested in learning this craft, learn about the materials, their usage, and much more through this chapter.

1.1 Essential Tools and Equipment

Any work or hobby you choose to spend time on has a few basic things you must adhere to when starting out. If you are interested in making crochet yourself, gather these essential things before starting out. These tools will be most necessary for you in crochet-making.

They are as follows:

Crochet Hooks

Crocheting requires one hook to work in contrast to knitting, which requires two needles to work together harmoniously. The hooks can be of various sizes and materials. You can choose which hook suits you best by trying a few different types, from steel, plastic, wood, aluminum, and bamboo.

As for the size, they all work best with their type of yarn thread. We will discuss how to select the yarn and hooks in the next section for better clarity. You may start with the size H-8 (5.00 mm), which can help you get to know the process of crocheting intimately with ease.

Here is a chart that conveys the sizes of hooks in the best manner:

CONVERSION CHART

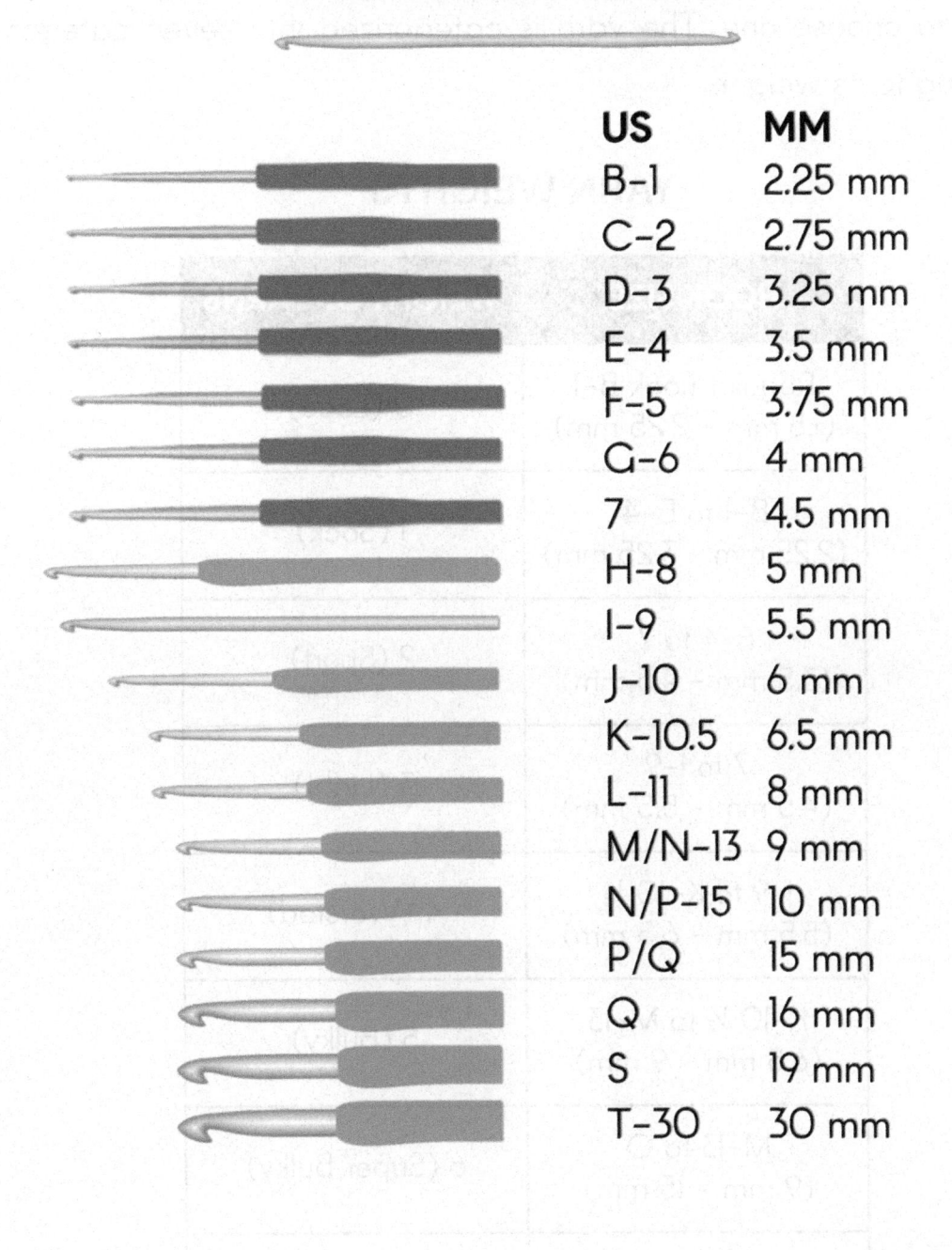

US	MM
B-1	2.25 mm
C-2	2.75 mm
D-3	3.25 mm
E-4	3.5 mm
F-5	3.75 mm
G-6	4 mm
7	4.5 mm
H-8	5 mm
I-9	5.5 mm
J-10	6 mm
K-10.5	6.5 mm
L-11	8 mm
M/N-13	9 mm
N/P-15	10 mm
P/Q	15 mm
Q	16 mm
S	19 mm
T-30	30 mm

Yarn

Yarns, like clothes, are multi-colored and textured, which makes it difficult to choose one. The yarn is categorized into seven categories according to its weight.

YARN WEIGHTS

HOOK SIZE	WEIGHT OF YARNS
Regular hook B-1 (1.5 mm – 2.25 mm)	0 (Lace)
B-1 to E-4 (2.25 mm – 3.25 mm)	1 (Sock)
E-4 to 7 (3.5 mm – 4.5 mm)	2 (Sport)
7 to I-9 (4.5 mm – 5.5 mm)	3 (Light)
I-9 to K-10 ½ (5.5 mm – 6.5 mm)	4 (Worsted)
K-10 ½ to M-13 (6.5 mm – 9 mm)	5 (Bulky)
M-13 to Q (9 mm – 15 mm)	6 (Super Bulky)
Q and larger (15 mm +)	7 (Jumbo)

In the beginning, I recommend going for number 4 or 5 for the yarn weight and finding a light-colored wool or wool-blended yarn (because they are easier to handle in comparison to cotton) to easily see and detect the errors. Any yarn that has a smooth and light texture should be good. Once you get the hang of the crocheting techniques, you can move on to more delicate or textured items.

Yarn Needle

Yarn needles have a few more names that can be used, such as tapestry or darning needles. The yarn needles are used to join the seams, motifs, and finishing various pieces.

They have two types of ends; some come with straight ends and others with bent ones.

You can choose which ever gets the job done according to the thickness of your yarn.

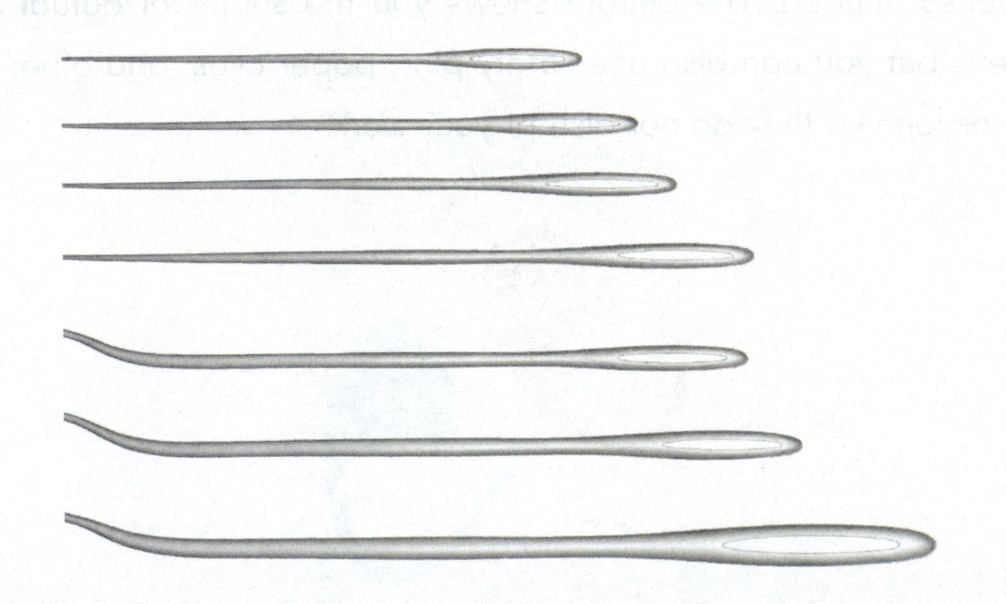

Scissors

Any type of scissors can be used for crocheting. You will only need to cut yarn or trim the ending with it, but you may get a small one to fit into a crochet bag or kit easily.

Stitch Markers

Stitch markers are important to remember the placements of stitches, especially in the learning phase. They help you in keeping your undivided attention on the task while maintaining the count and number of stitches needed. The picture shows you the shape of actual stitch markers, but you can also use safety pins, paper clips, and other such items as long as they do not disrupt your work.

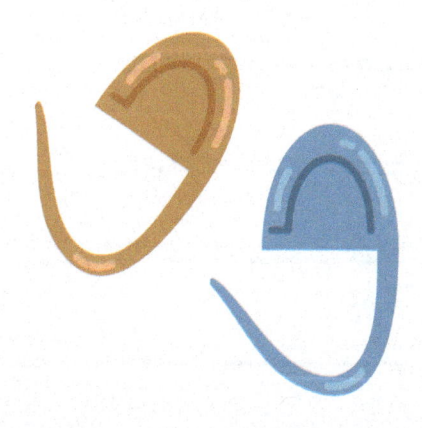

MEASURING TAPE

Measurement tape is another important item that is a must for crochet beginners. It helps you measure the pieces as you move along to see how it all works. You can use a standard measuring tape, as shown in the picture, or buy a retraceable one.

On one side of the tape, you will find measurement in inches and in centimeters on the other side. The numbers have bigger lines to denote their placement, while the semi-long line in between two numbers denotes the half-way point.

Simply put the tape on whatever you wish to measure, and put the starting end on the starting point. Tighten the tape a bit to get an accurate measurement every time.

Other things you may need for ease but not out of necessity:

- Row Counter
- Crochet Project Bag or Tote
- Crochet Hook Case
- Swatch Ruler and Hook Gauge
- Blocking Mats and Pins

1.2 Choosing the Right Yarn and Hooks

Whether it is yarn or hook, you need to make sure they are compatible by looking at their size and compatibility with each other. Whenever you buy a yarn, the first thing you do is figure out which size of hook is best for it. If you have a complete set of hooks at home, it's fine. But if you need a yarn that matches the hook, look at the labels to find the best match.

Consult the Yarn Weight Chart in heading 1.1.2 (page no.12) to have the complete picture of the compatible sizes.

Choosing Yarn

Yarns come in many shapes and forms. It is best to get familiar with the shapes of yarn and how they are different from each other.

Keep in Mind!

The shape of yarn doesn't change its quality, color, or other properties. They are just different in terms of usage in making various items.

SKEIN has a cylindrical shape, and you can pull out the yarn from the inside or outside for usage. It can lose its shape when you have used more than half of it. For smooth and tangle-free usage, simply roll the remaining yarn into a ball to stay taut.

HANK is just another way of tying and storing the yarn. A hank is best for keeping or shipping the yarn. It is visually appealing, but in use, you will need to wind it up into a ball before starting your project.

A BALL is definitely the most convenient shape for the yarn. It is easy to use, and most of the time, all types of packaging need to be reduced to this one. This type of yarn can be pulled from both inside and outside, according to the need and use.

THE CAKE is aptly named for its flat-top shape, which makes it unique. It is packaged in this way to stop the bundled yarn from rolling around or losing shape. It is also very popular because of the convenience of pulling the yarn from the inside.

In terms of finding the appropriate material, it is best to start with wool (either pure or mixed) because it is the easiest to work with. But you can also use cotton, acrylic, and natural and synthetic mixes.

Once you are familiar with the shapes and materials, it is essential to discuss the yarn labels. They may seem inconsequential at the time of purchase, but they contain a lot of important information that may be beneficial for newbies like you.

Always save your labels, even when you start crocheting, because they will let you know about essential instructions to keep in mind. Use the symbols provided here as a guidance cheat sheet to know which sign indicates what on a ball band.

> ### Did You Know?
> Ball Band is the band that secures the yarns stored in any shape. It contains the label name and information that is crucial to know for proper usage.

These important symbols and information can be used later to buy the same color, size, material, etc., to finish the project.

Yarn Weight and Thickness	Recommended Hook Size	Gauge over a 4in (10 cm) Test Square

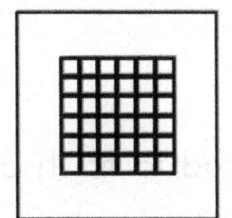

Shade/Color Number	 Dye Lot Number	Weight of Ball of Yarn	Fiber Content
Machine-Wash Cold	Machine-Wash Cold Gentle Cycle	Hand-Wash Cold	Hand-Wash Warm
Do Not Bleach	Dry-Cleanable in Any Solvent	Dry-Cleanable in Certain Solvents	Do Not Dry-Clean
Do Not Tumble-Dry	Do Not Iron	Iron on Low Heat	Iron on Medium Heat

> **TIP!**
>
> If you need to finish a project and yarn runs out, try to find the same dye lot number again in yarn to avoid any color differences. Or, best yet, buy more than the calculated need. You can always use it later for something smaller.

HOLDING THE YARN

The yarn has to stay tight and tangle-free to keep the project going steady and easy. For that reason, use the yarn string as shown here.

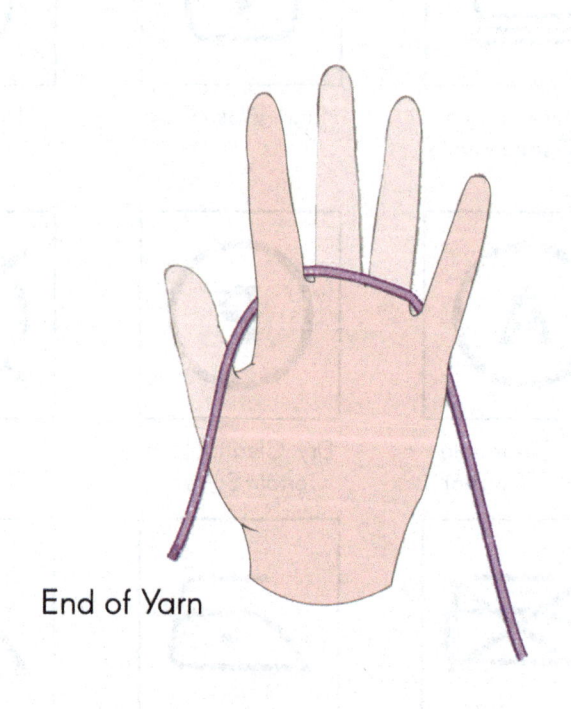

End of Yarn

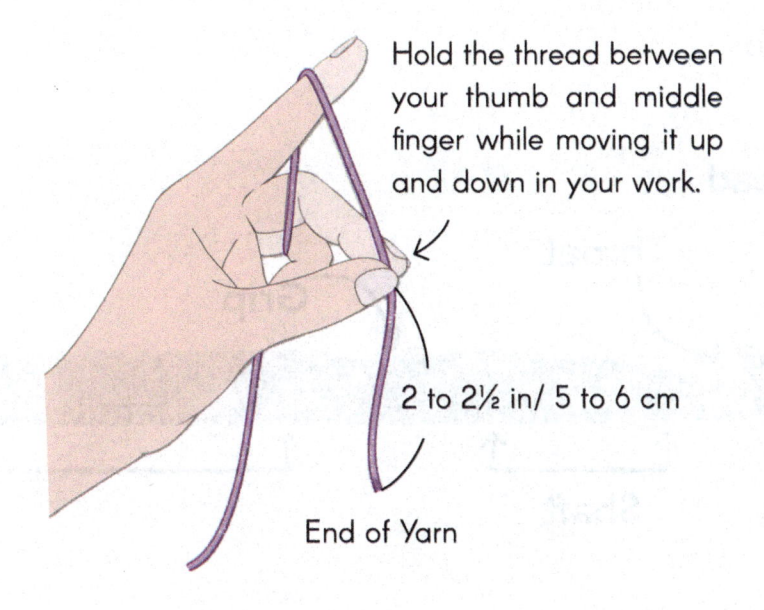

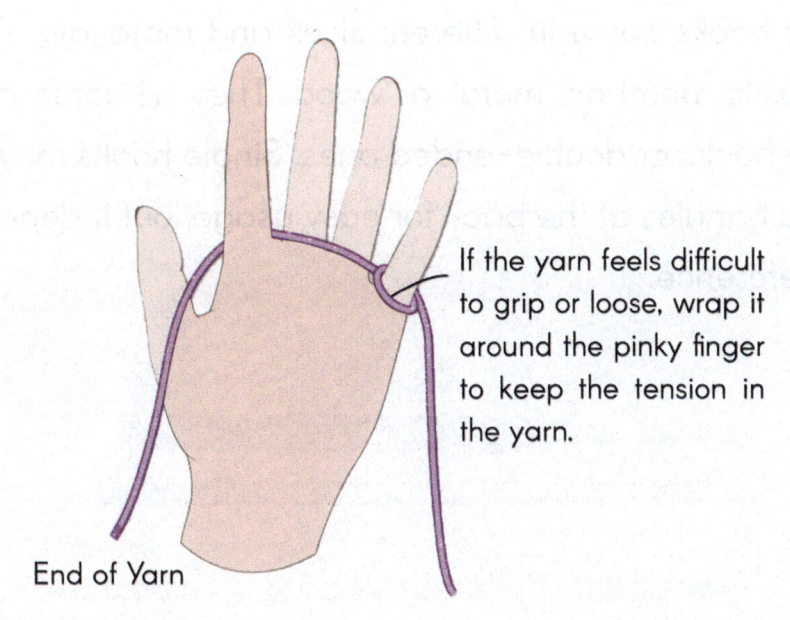

Hold the thread between your thumb and middle finger while moving it up and down in your work.

2 to 2½ in/ 5 to 6 cm

End of Yarn

If the yarn feels difficult to grip or loose, wrap it around the pinky finger to keep the tension in the yarn.

End of Yarn

Choosing Hooks

Let us first look at the anatomy of a hook to know the names of all parts for better usage and understanding later on.

It is labeled as:

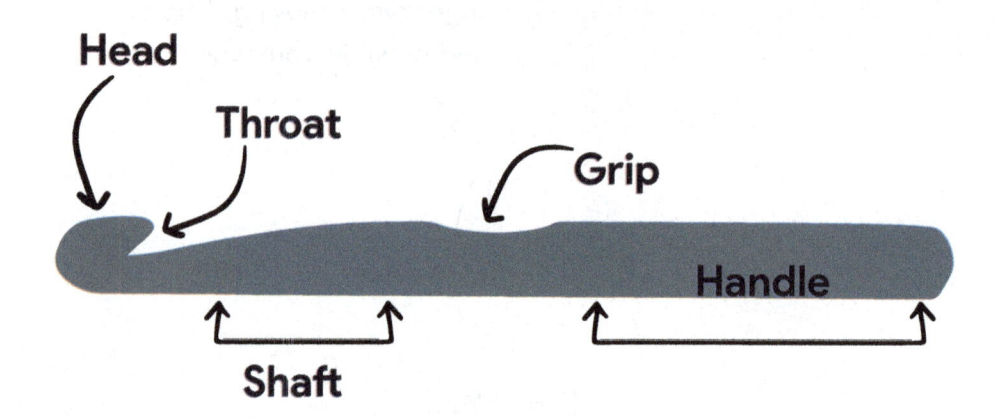

Head **Throat** **Grip**

Handle

Shaft

The crochet hooks come in different sizes and materials. They can be made of plastic, bamboo, metal, or wood. They all come in two types: Either single hooks or double-ended ones. Single hooks may or may not have coated handles at the back for easy usage, but it depends on your personal preference.

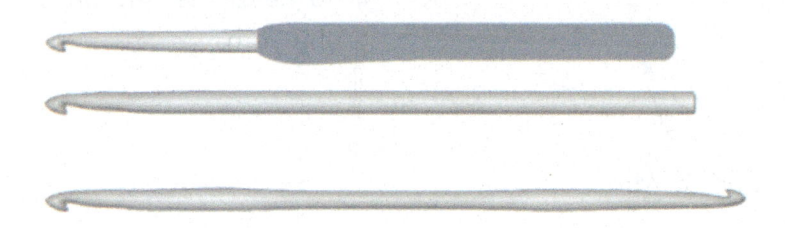

By now, you know that the regular hooks have different and bigger sizes from the lace hooks. They are usually steel hooks with smaller head sizes. As they get thinner in size, their number increases. With lace hooks, you can make tighter and more refined designs, while the regular hooks will help you with open-weave designs that are much bulkier.

Lace Hooks

12
10
8
6
4
2
0

Regular Hooks

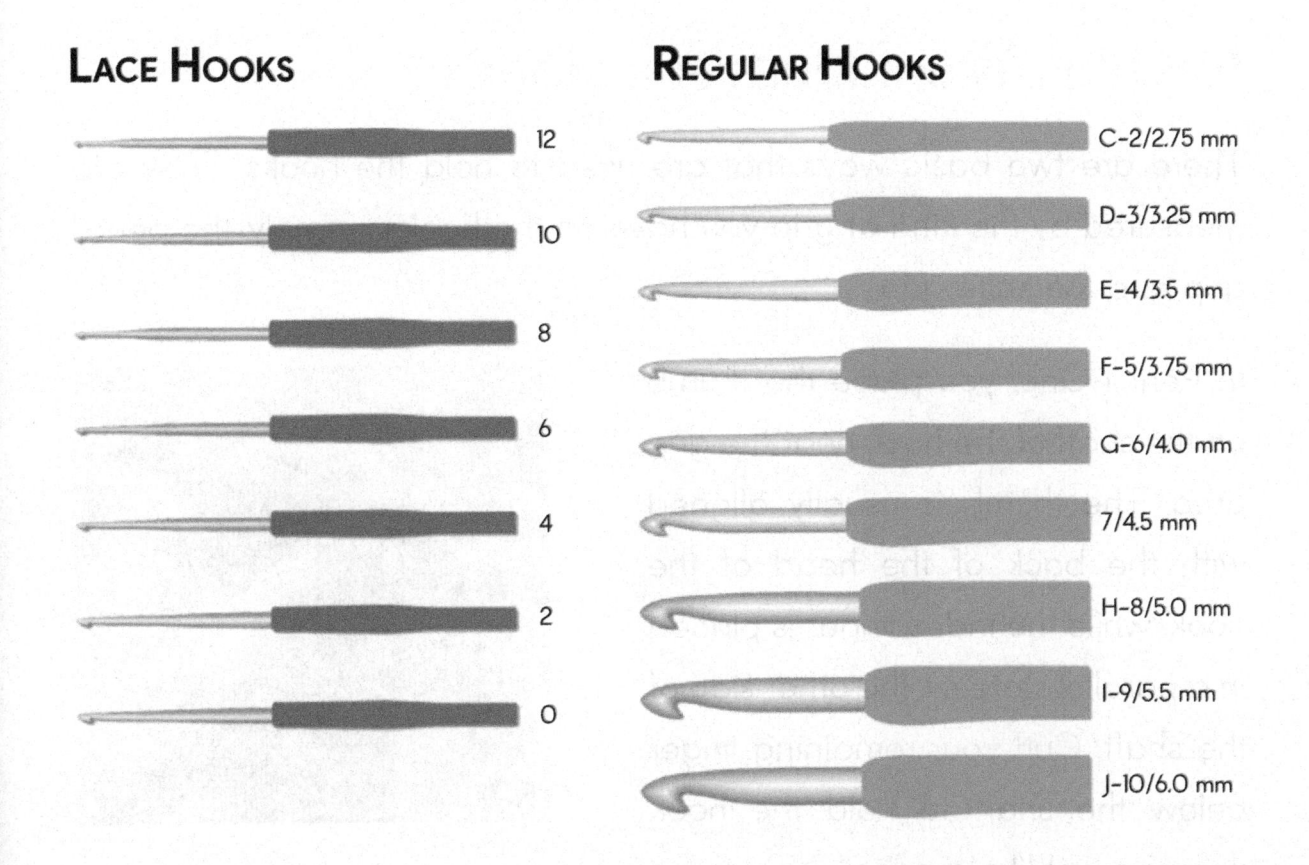

C-2/2.75 mm
D-3/3.25 mm
E-4/3.5 mm
F-5/3.75 mm
G-6/4.0 mm
7/4.5 mm
H-8/5.0 mm
I-9/5.5 mm
J-10/6.0 mm

It is best to use the hook size as indicated on the label. It will help you avoid much hassle, especially as a beginner.

HOLDING TECHNIQUES FOR HOOKS

There are two basic ways that are used to hold the hooks. They are measured by the kind of grip you have on the hooks, namely, the pencil grip and the knife grip.

In Pencil Grip, you place the thumb on the shaft of the hook near the grip area. The thumb is usually aligned with the back of the head of the hook, while the index finger is placed in a parallel state on the other side of the shaft. Curl your remaining finger below the shaft to hold the hook properly, just like a pencil.

In Knife Grip, use your thumb and middle finger to hold the hook. The head should be faced down, while the index finger should be placed straight ahead with a little bend, as shown in the picture.

Out of these two methods, you can use any method that works well for you. If you are comfortable with the setting, you may start the crocheting. Although these are the standard grips, finding a placement that allows you to stay in control while working smoothly is best.

Here is how you can use the hook with the pencil grip (the last image shows the last position of holding yarn with the hook):

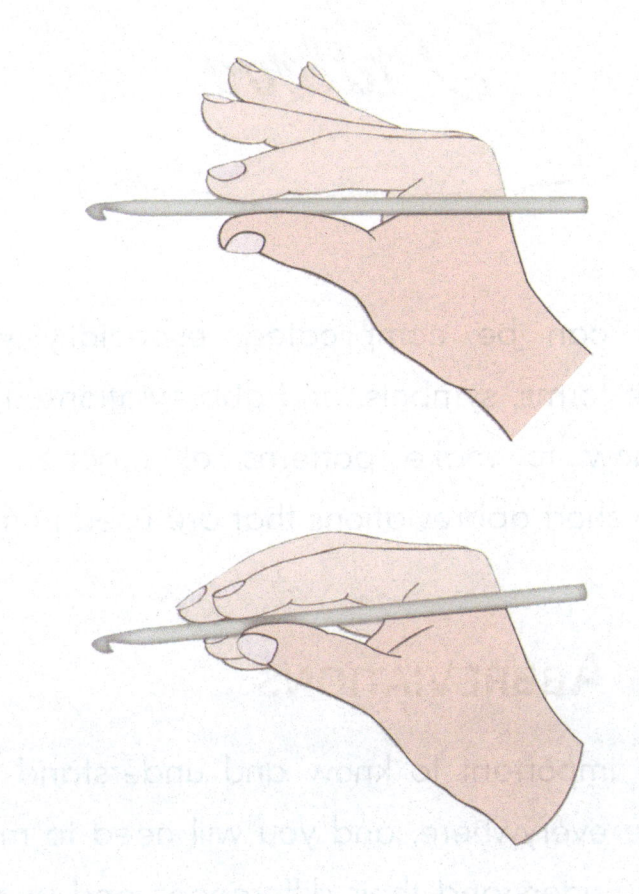

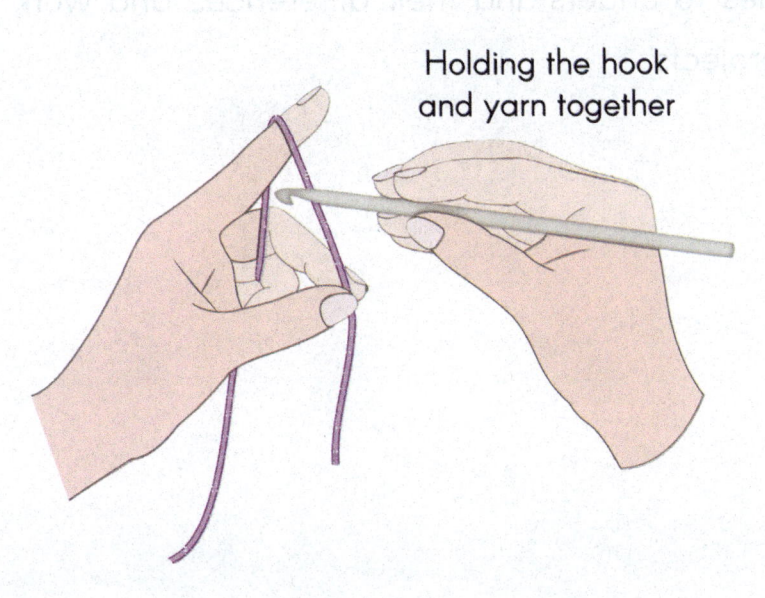

Holding the hook and yarn together

1.3 Understanding Crochet Patterns

Crochet patterns can be complicated, especially when you are unfamiliar with the terms, symbols, and abbreviations. This section will guide you on how to make patterns of crochet that work by understanding the short abbreviations that are used in most crocheting projects.

DECIPHERING ABBREVIATIONS

Abbreviations are important to know and understand in the crochet business. They are everywhere, and you will need to memorize a few important ones to understand their differences and work smoothly on your future projects.

Abbreviation	Description
alt	alternate
approx	approximately
beg	begin/beginning
bet	between
BL or BLO	back loop or back loop only
bo	bobble
BP	back post
BPdc	back post double crochet
BPdtr	back post double treble crochet
BPhdc	back post half double crochet
BPsc	back post single crochet
BPtr	back post treble crochet
CC	contrasting color
ch	chain stitch
ch-	refer to chain or space previously made, e.g., ch-1 space
ch-sp	chain space
CL	cluster
cont	continue
dc	double crochet

dc2tog	double crochet 2 stitches together
dec	decrease
dtr	double treble crochet
edc	extended double crochet
ehdc	extended half double crochet
esc	extended single crochet
etr	extended treble crochet
FL or FLO	front loop or front loop only
foll	following
FP	front post
FPdc	front post double crochet
FPdtr	front post double treble crochet
FPhdc	front post half double crochet
FPsc	front post single crochet
FPtr	front post treble crochet
hdc	half double crochet
hdc2tog	half double crochet 2 stitches together
inc	increase
lp	loop
m	marker
MC	main color

pat or patt	pattern
pc	popcorn stitch
pm	place marker
prev	previous
ps or puff	puff stitch
rem	remaining
rep	repeat
rnd	round
RS	right side
sc	single crochet
sc2tog	single crochet 2 stitches together
sh	shell
sk	skip
sl st	slip stitch
sl or sl m	slip marker
sp	space
st	stitch
tbl	through back loop
tch or t-ch	turning chain
tog	together
tr	treble crochet

tr2tog	treble crochet 2 stitches together
trtr	triple treble crochet
WS	wrong side
yo	yarn over
Yoh	yarn over hook

Terms & Common Measurements

These are a few terms and measurements that are common in crochet. They will also guide you in reading the instructions better and measuring the raw materials or projects that are in the works.

Term	Description
*	repeat the instructions following the single asterisk as directed
* *	repeat instructions between asterisks as many times as directed or repeat at specified locations
{ }	work instructions within brackets as many times as directed
[ ]	work instructions within brackets as many times as directed
( )	work instructions within parentheses as many times as directed or work a group of stitches all in the same stitch or space

Measurement	Description
" or in	inch
cm	centimeter
g	gram
m	meter
mm	millimeter
oz	ounce
yd	yard

ABBREVIATION & TERM DIFFERENCES BETWEEN THE U.S. AND U.K.

The US and UK versions of stitches and basic terms can differ from each other and cause confusion. We will be using US terms throughout the book, but you can consult this chart whenever you encounter the UK terms.

U.S./Canada	U.K.
slip stitch (sl st)	slip stitch (ss)
single crochet (sc)	double crochet (dc)
half double crochet (hdc)	half treble (htr)
double crochet (dc)	treble (tr)

U.S./Canada	U.K.
treble (tr)	double treble (dtr)
double treble (dtr)	triple treble (trtr)
gauge	tension
yarn over (yo)	yarn over hook (yoh)

Reading Chart Patterns

When it comes to reading charts of crochet patterns, it is best to consult the signs that indicate the patterns. It will tell you about the type and number of stitches being used.

Let's look at the symbols first:

SYMBOL	DESCRIPTION
⬓	Chain (ch)
⋏	Slip stitch (ss)
⋔	Single crochet (sc)
⬓	Half double crochet (hdc)
⬓	Double crochet (dc)
V	Treble crochet (tr)

SYMBOL	DESCRIPTION
(double treble symbol)	Double treble crochet (dtr)
(sc2tog symbol)	Single crochet 2 together (sc2tog)
(sc3tog symbol)	Single crochet 3 together (sc3tog)
○	ch-3 picot
●	3 hdc cluster/puff st/bobble
X or +	Double crochet 2 together (dc2tog)
T	Double crochet 3 together (dc3tog)
T	3-dc cluster
T	5-dc popcorn
T	Double crochet increase (dc inc)
∧	5-dc shell
∧	Back post dc (BPdc)
(FPdc symbol)	Front post double crochet (FPdc)

When these symbols are used in harmony to create a pattern, they make a sophisticated array of symbols that tell us how and which stitches have made the pattern.

Chapter 2

Basic Stitches

After learning about the crochet basics, it is time to discuss the basic stitches that are used most commonly and need to be mastered by crochet beginners. Once you are familiar with the working of these stitches, you will find it much easier to incorporate other patterns into your practices and projects.

2.1 The Slip Knot

The slip knot is not one of the stitches but a primary starting point that is used not only in crocheting but knitting as well.

Here is how you do it:

1.

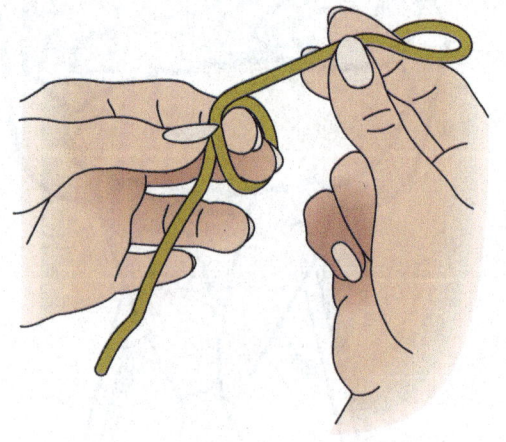

Make a circle from the yarn that loops around two of your fingers.

2.

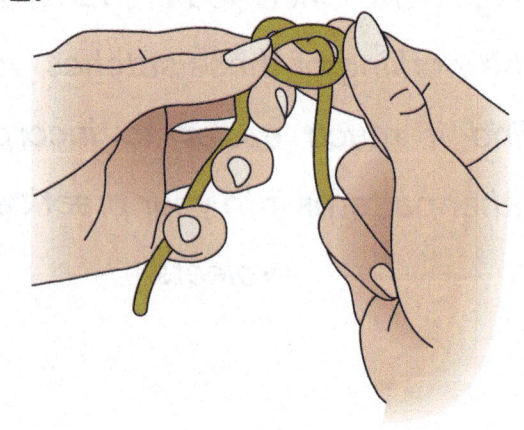

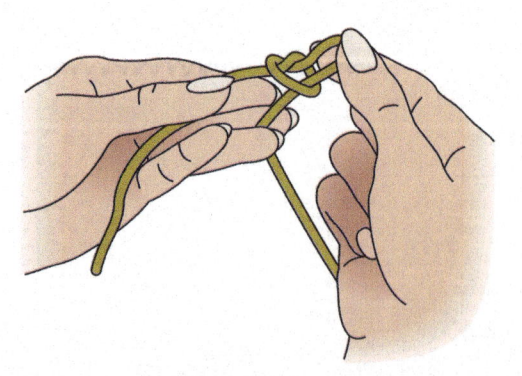

Pull out a loop from that circle.

3.

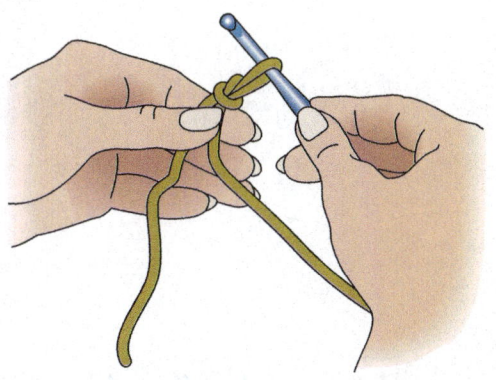

In that pulled loop, insert the hook.

4.

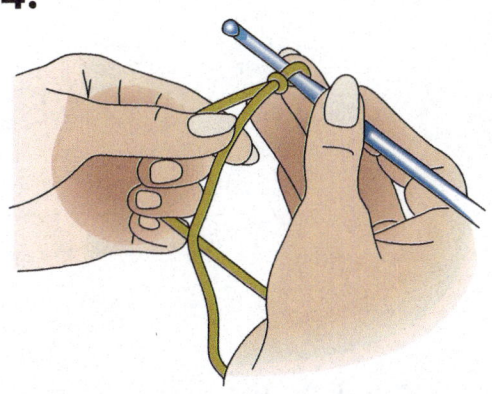

Tighten the yarn around the hook till it is securely wrapped around.

Yarn Over (yo)

The yarn over technique is quite often used in crocheting. It involves the simple step; you need to bring the yarn from back to front by looping it over the hook. The yarn should stay taut to have the same tension in your project.

Yarn Over (yo)

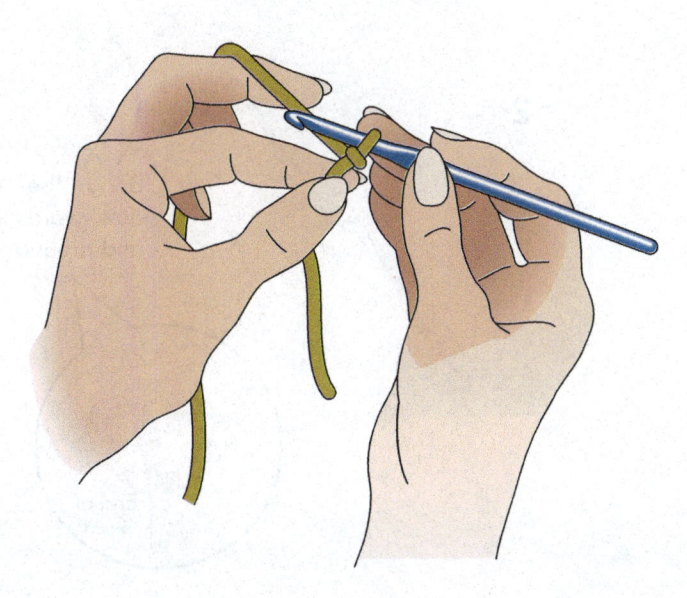

2.2 - The Chain Stitch

Chain Stitch is the most basic stitch you need to master first. Use the instructions to follow along.

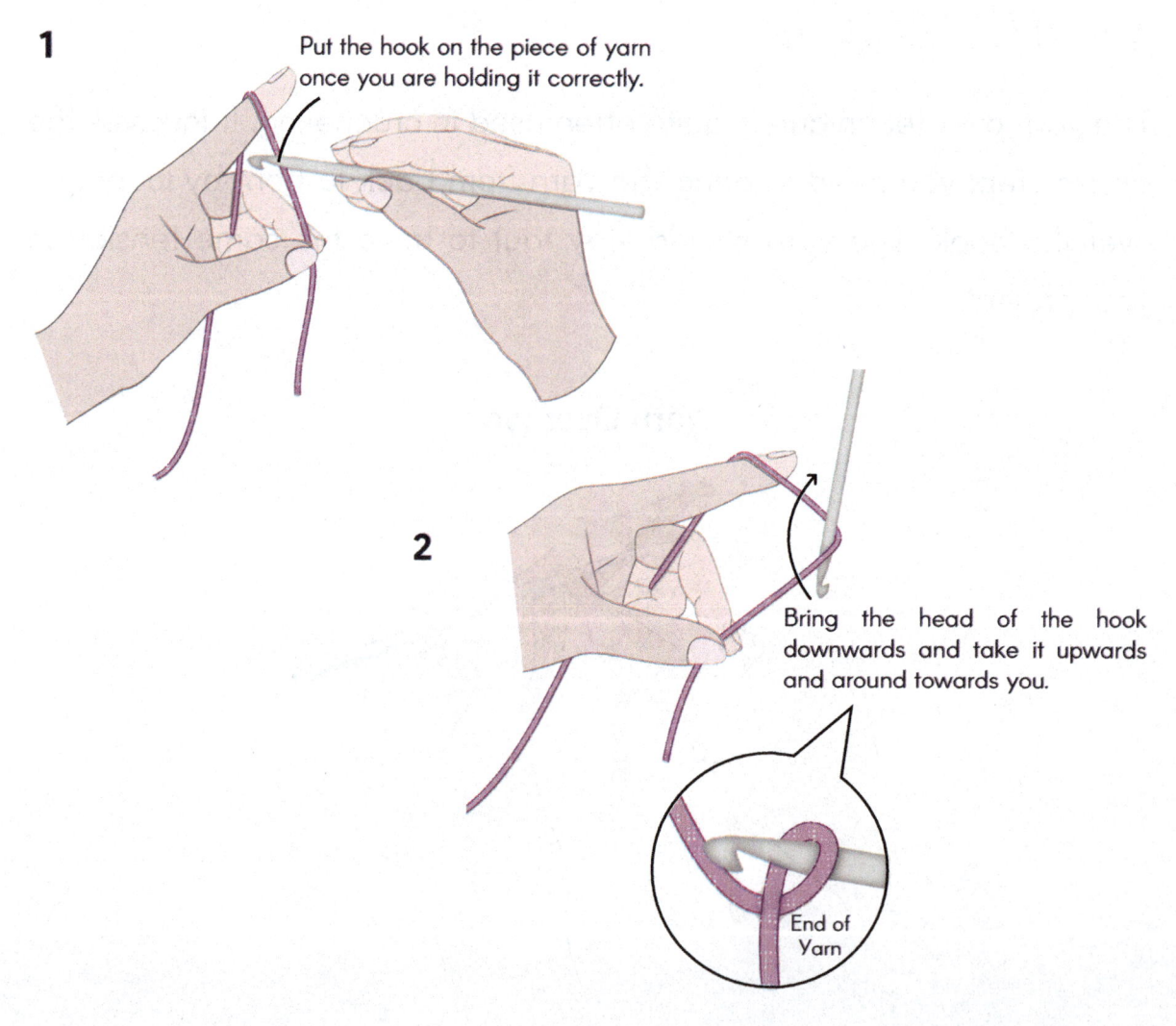

1 Put the hook on the piece of yarn once you are holding it correctly.

2 Bring the head of the hook downwards and take it upwards and around towards you.

End of Yarn

3

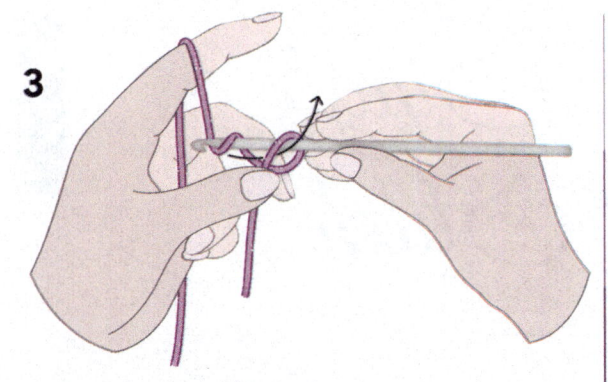

Now, wrap the hook where you can see the yarn twisting.

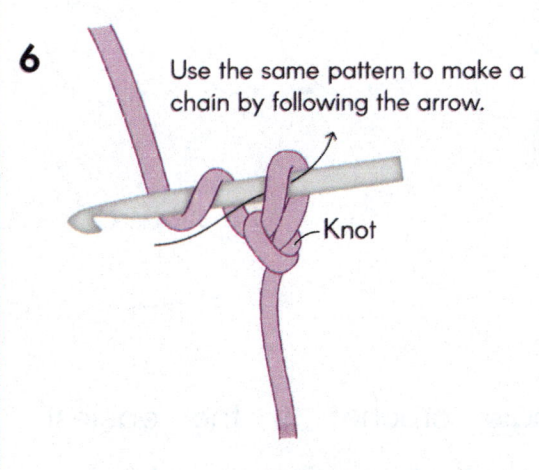

4

5

It should form a slipknot now.

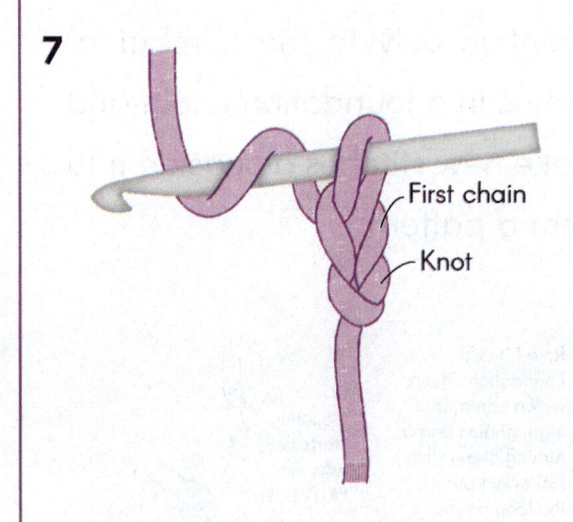

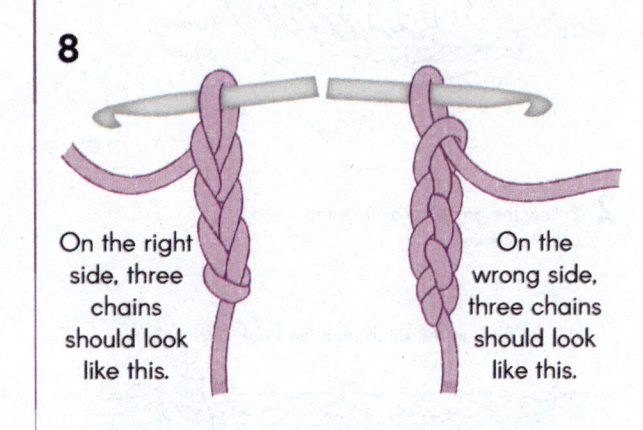

6 Use the same pattern to make a chain by following the arrow.

Knot

7

First chain

Knot

8

On the right side, three chains should look like this.

On the wrong side, three chains should look like this.

2.3 The Single Crochet Stitch

Single crochet is the easiest stitch that requires you to pay attention only to the number of chains in a foundation chain and make new stitches alongside it to form a pattern.

> **REMEMBER!**
>
> Slipknots are not counted as a stitch in crocheting.

1 Row 1 has a Foundation Chain, which contains eight chains and a turning chain (the last chain before the loop on the hook).

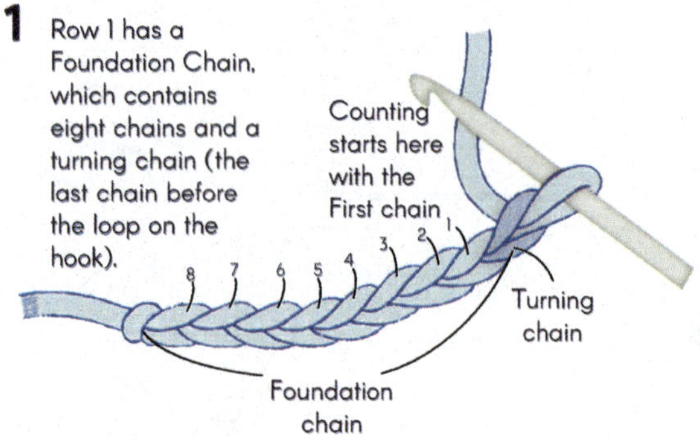

Counting starts here with the First chain
Turning chain
Foundation chain

2 Follow the arrow's movement to link the chains.

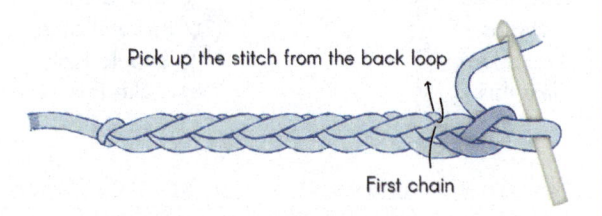

Pick up the stitch from the back loop
First chain

2(a) Insert hook here

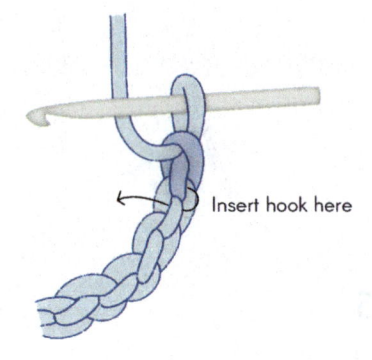

2(b)

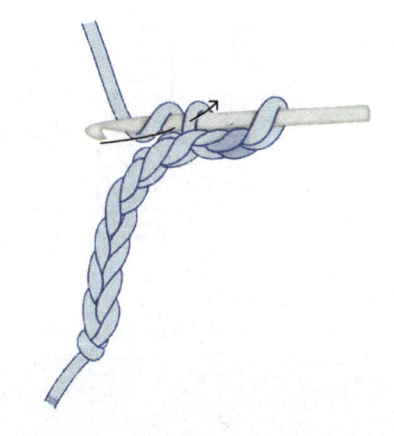

3 Make one single crochet by bringing the hook through the loops.

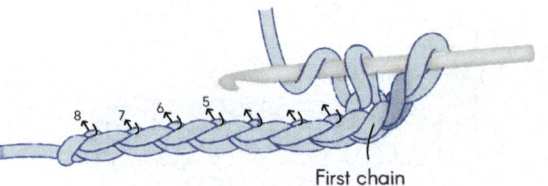

8 7 6 5
First chain

4 This is what your First single crochet should look like.

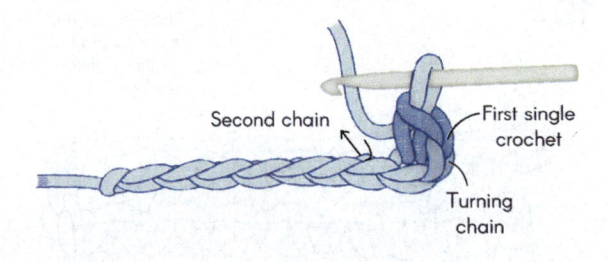

Second chain — First single crochet
Turning chain

5 Repeat the same process until the eight single crochet stitches are made.

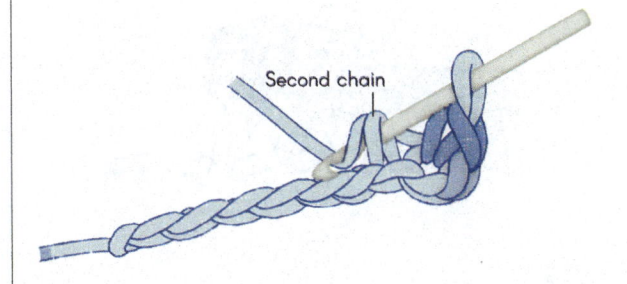

Second chain

6 This is how your first row should look after completion.

8 7 6 5 4 3 2   First single crochet

If you want to keep practicing, repeat the same process for Rows 2 & 3.

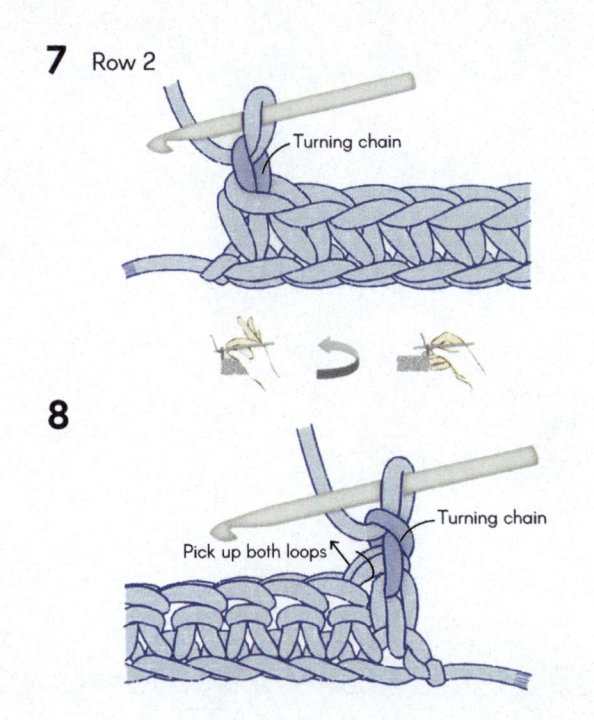

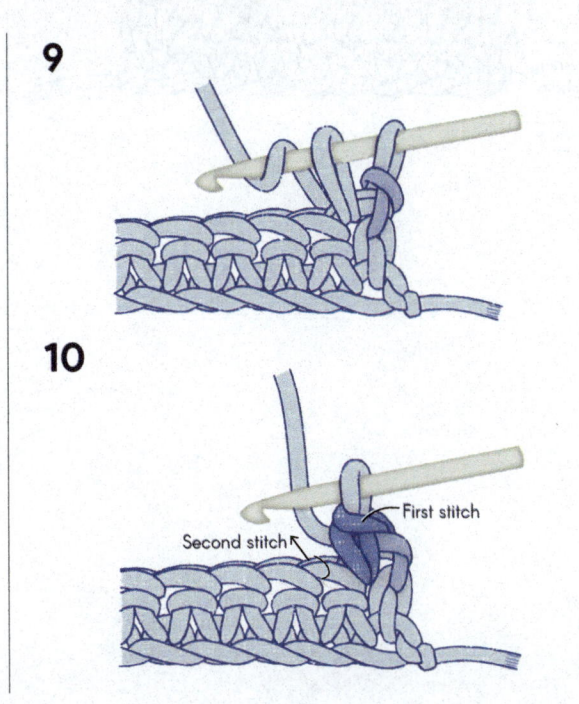

7 Row 2

Turning chain

8

Pick up both loops — Turning chain

9

10

Second stitch — First stitch

41

11

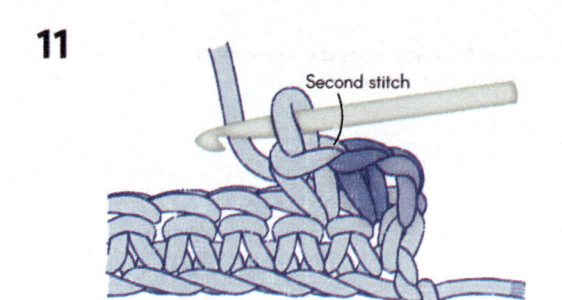

Second stitch

12

Eighth stitch
Turning chain, Row 1

13

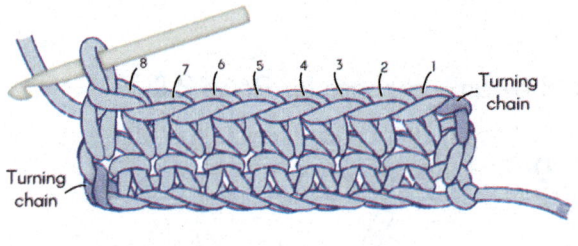

8 7 6 5 4 3 2 1 Turning chain

Turning chain

14 Row 3

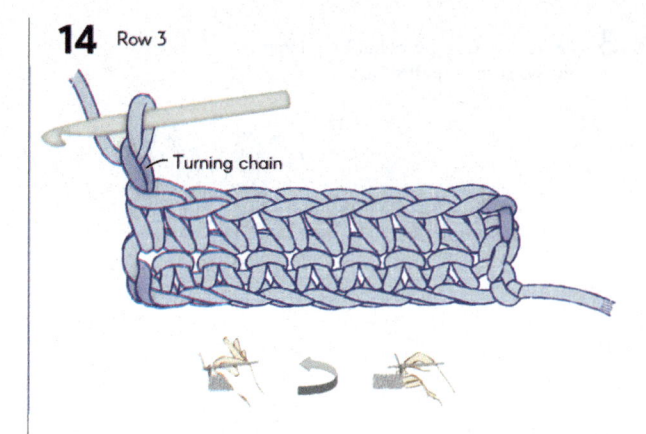

Turning chain

15

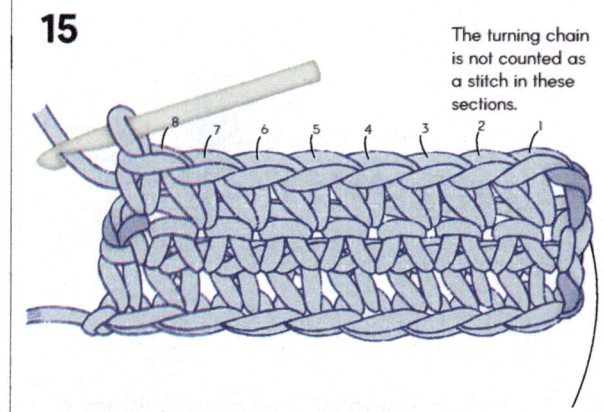

8 7 6 5 4 3 2 1

The turning chain is not counted as a stitch in these sections.

2.4 The Double Crochet Stitch

The double crochet stitch has three chains in the turning chain. In Row 1, they will be counted as the first stitch. You can simply yarn over, insert the hook in the foundation chain, and pull up a loop (3 loops are on the hook). Then, you may yarn over again and pull the yarn through the two loops twice.

Follow the detailed instructions below to get the whole gist.

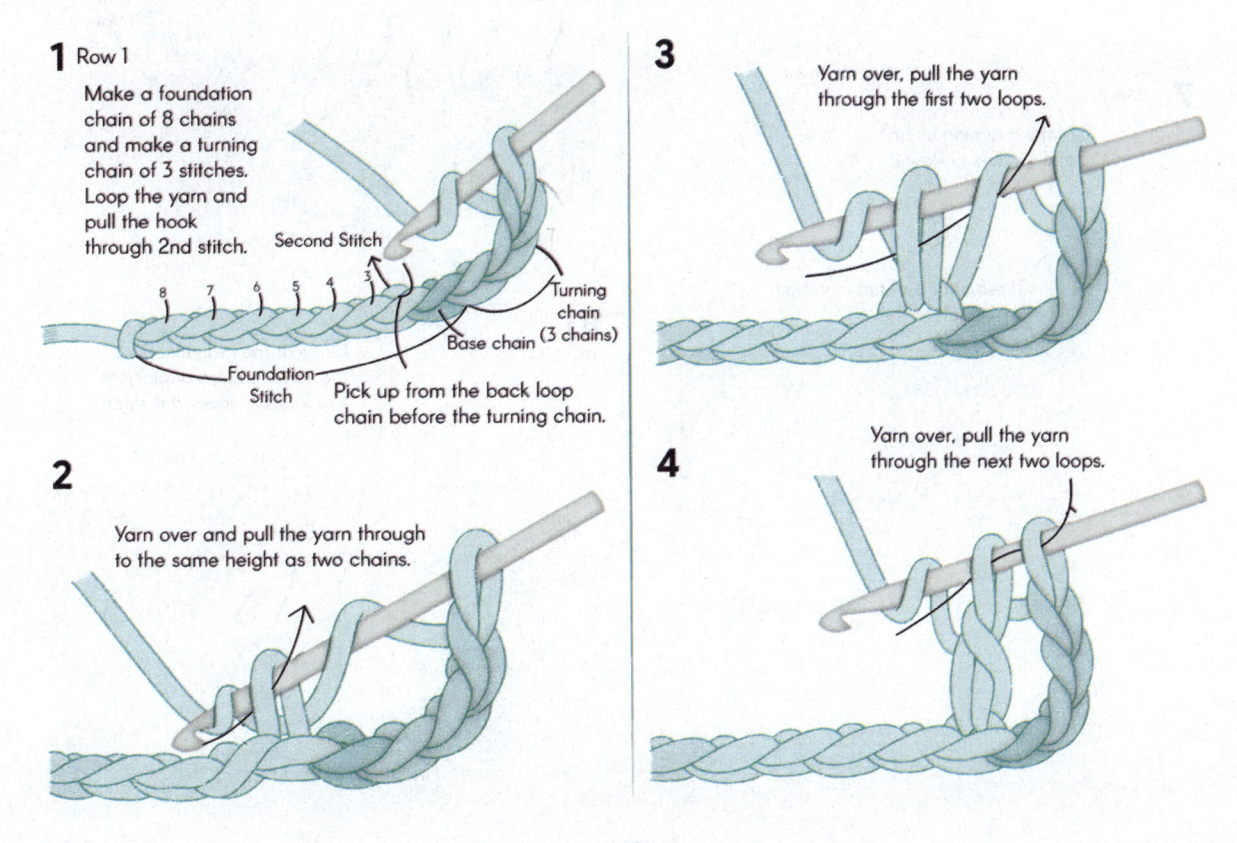

1 Row 1

Make a foundation chain of 8 chains and make a turning chain of 3 stitches. Loop the yarn and pull the hook through 2nd stitch.

Second Stitch
Turning chain (3 chains)
Base chain
Foundation Stitch
Pick up from the back loop chain before the turning chain.

2 Yarn over and pull the yarn through to the same height as two chains.

3 Yarn over, pull the yarn through the first two loops.

4 Yarn over, pull the yarn through the next two loops.

5

Repeat the same process for all eight chains.

Second Stitch
First Stitch
Turning chain
Base chain

6

Once complete, bring the hook through the last loop to make turning stitches.

First Stitch

7 Row 2

Make a turning chain of 3 stitches in Row 2.

Three chains of turning chain (first stitch of Row 2)

8

Yarn over and pick up from under two loops.

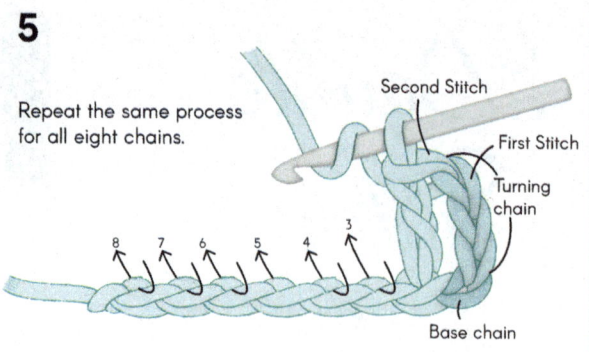

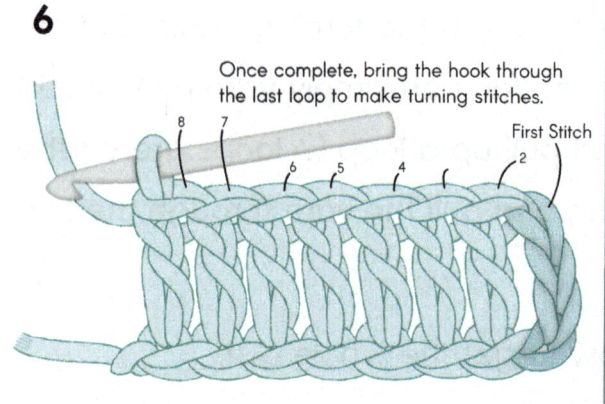

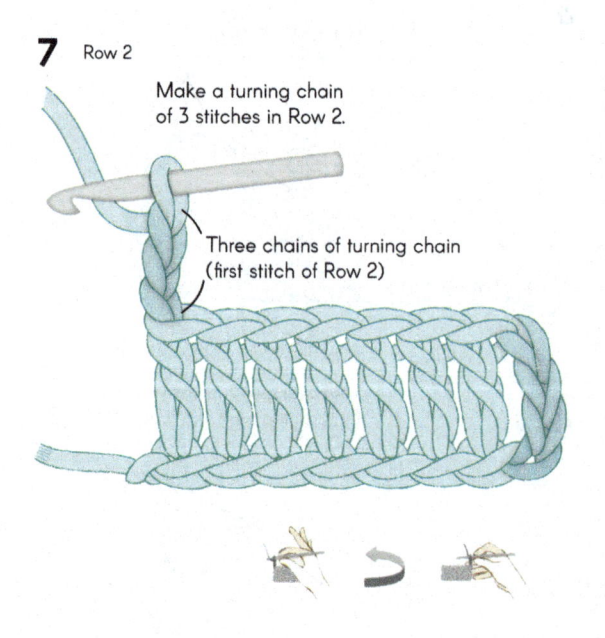

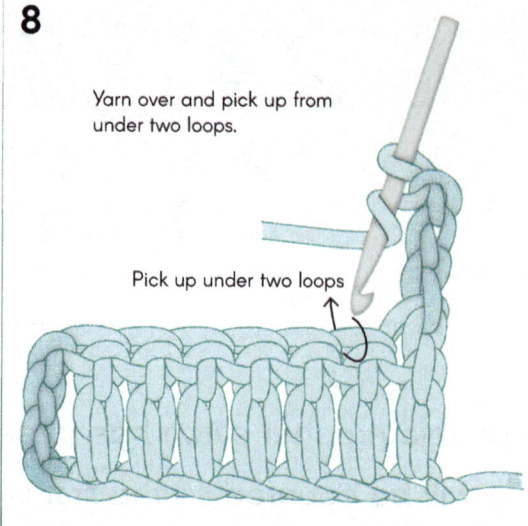

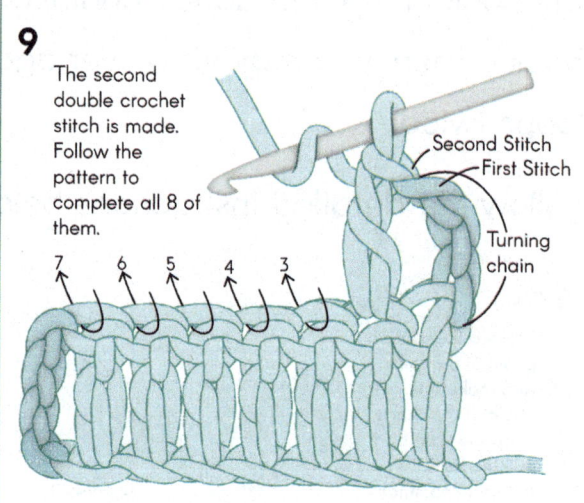

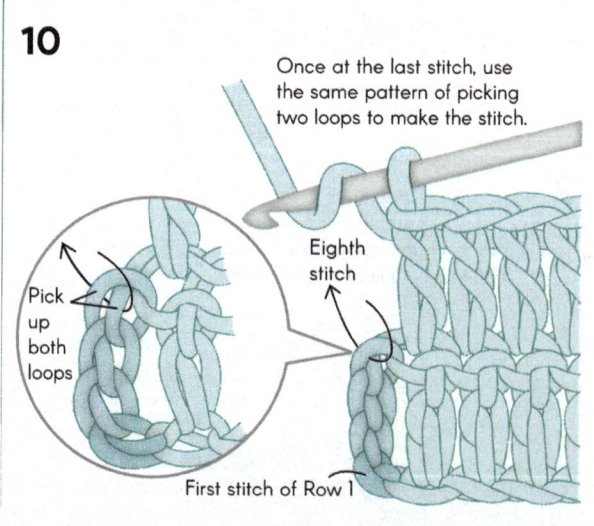

Pick up under two loops

9

The second double crochet stitch is made. Follow the pattern to complete all 8 of them.

Second Stitch
First Stitch
Turning chain

10

Once at the last stitch, use the same pattern of picking two loops to make the stitch.

Pick up both loops

Eighth stitch

First stitch of Row 1

44

11 Row 3

Repeat the same procedure you used to make rows 1 & 2.

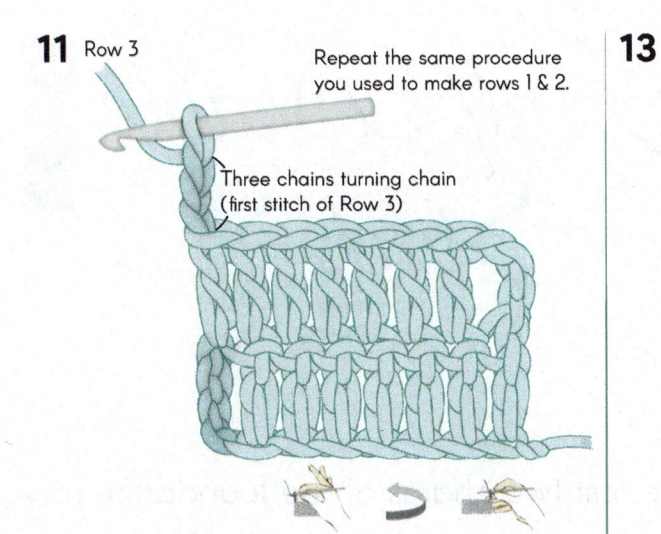

Three chains turning chain (first stitch of Row 3)

12

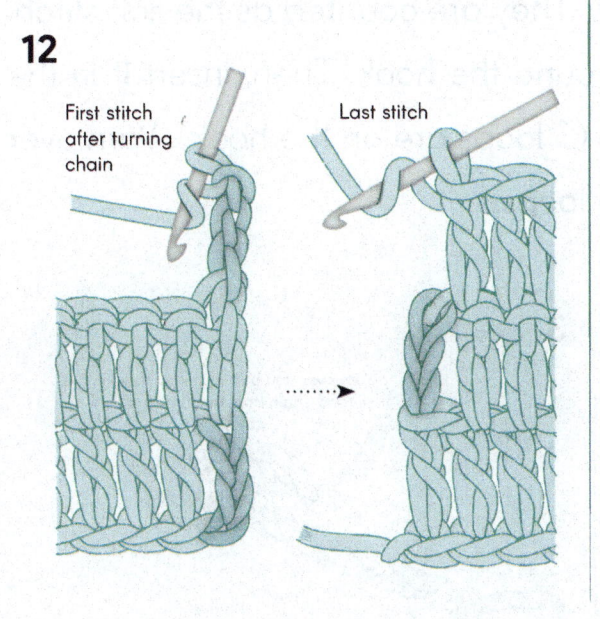

First stitch after turning chain

Last stitch

13

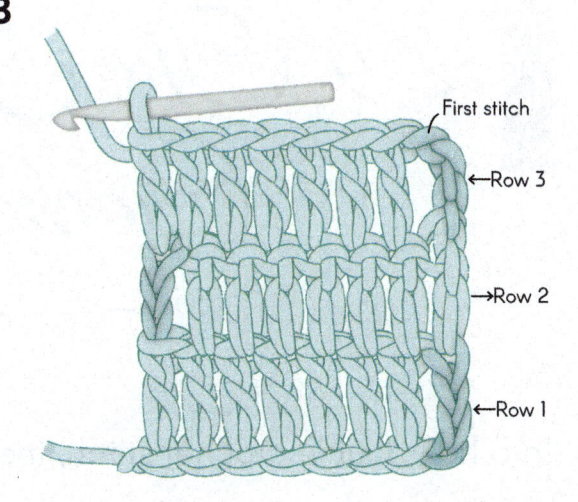

First stitch

←Row 3
→Row 2
←Row 1

45

2.5 The Half Double Crochet Stitch

In a half double crochet stitch, the first two chains of the foundation row are the turning chains of the first row. They are counted as the first stitch. You need to wrap the yarn once around the hook. Then, insert it in the foundation chain and pull up a loop (3 loops are on the hook). Yarn over and pull up a loop through all three loops.

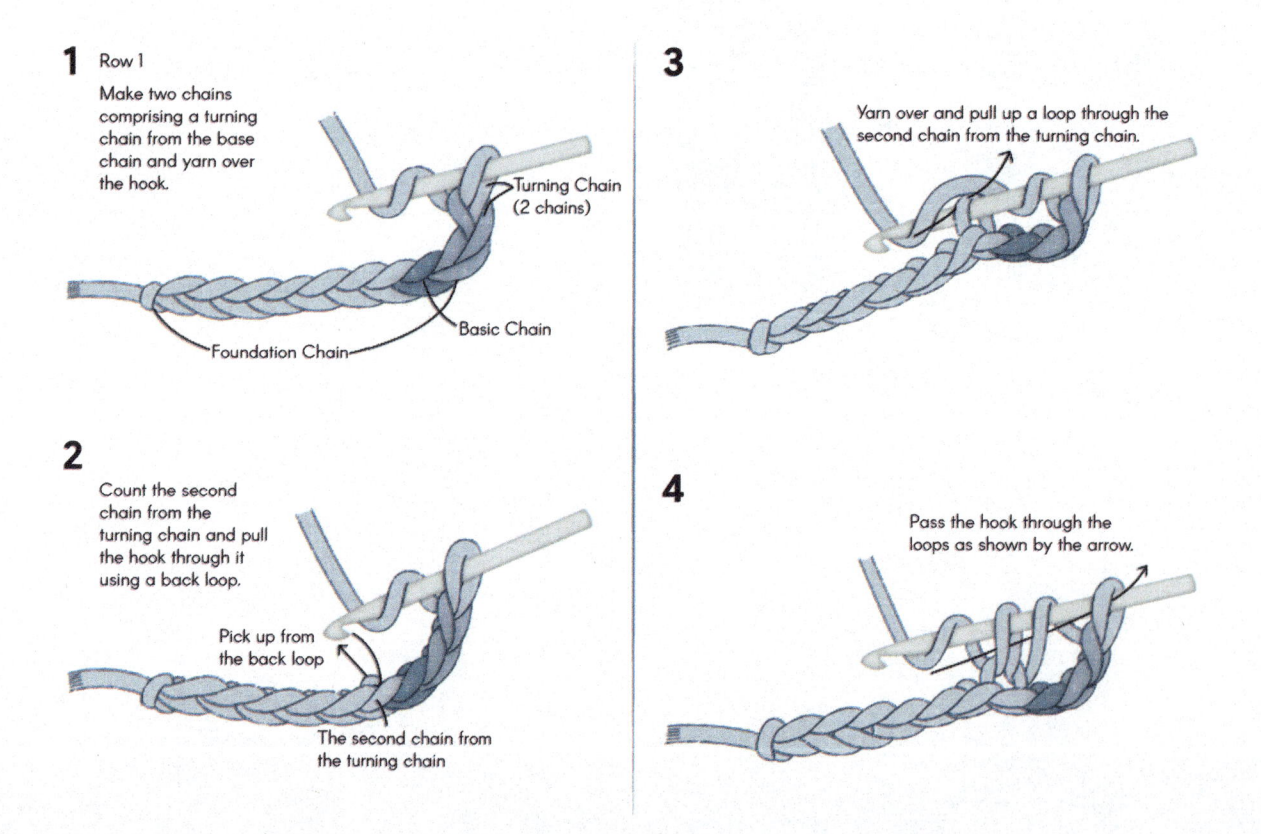

1 Row 1
Make two chains comprising a turning chain from the base chain and yarn over the hook.

Turning Chain (2 chains)
Basic Chain
Foundation Chain

2 Count the second chain from the turning chain and pull the hook through it using a back loop.

Pick up from the back loop
The second chain from the turning chain

3 Yarn over and pull up a loop through the second chain from the turning chain.

4 Pass the hook through the loops as shown by the arrow.

5 Once the second chain is in place, repeat the same pattern until the eighth and last chain.

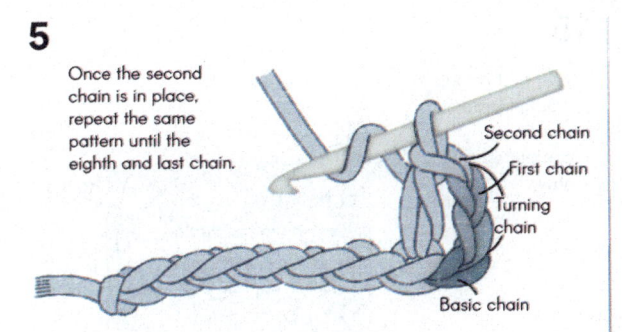

Second chain
First chain
Turning chain
Basic chain

6 Make the opening for the turning chain.

First stitch

7 Row 2
Make the turning chain with two chains.

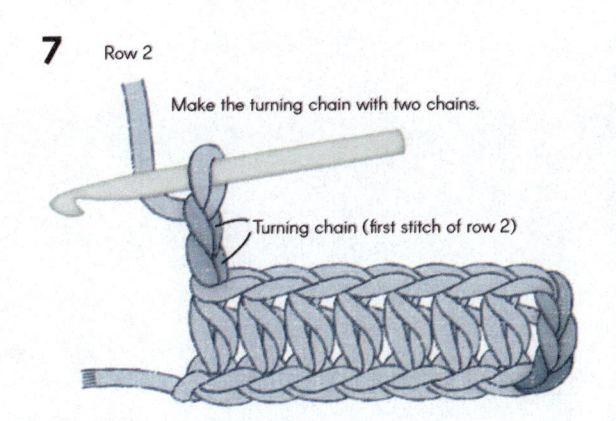

Turning chain (first stitch of row 2)

8 When the turning chain (first stitch) is made, yarn over the hook and pull it from two loops of the 2nd stitch.
Pick up under both loops

First stitch of Row 2

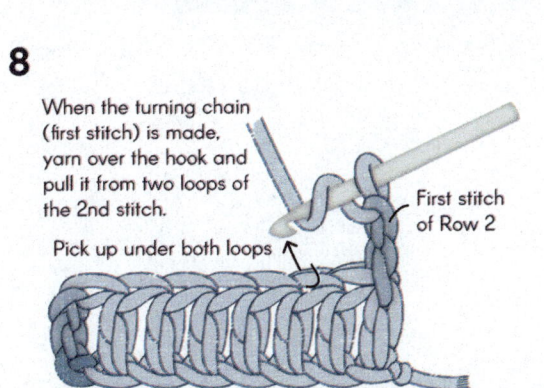

9 Yarn over the hook and pass it through the three loops as shown.

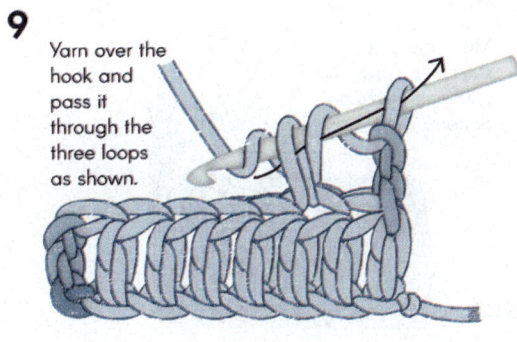

10 Repeat the same step for the whole row.

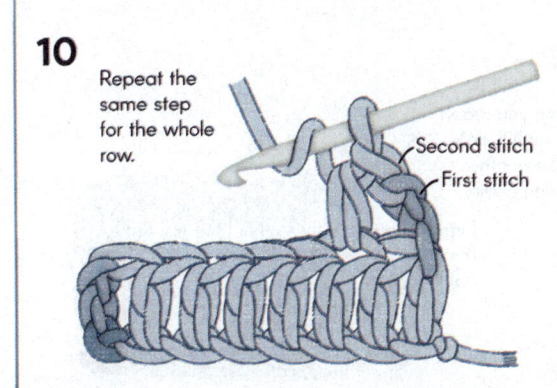

Second stitch
First stitch

11
Second stitch
Eighth stitch
Turning chain from first row (pick up both loops)

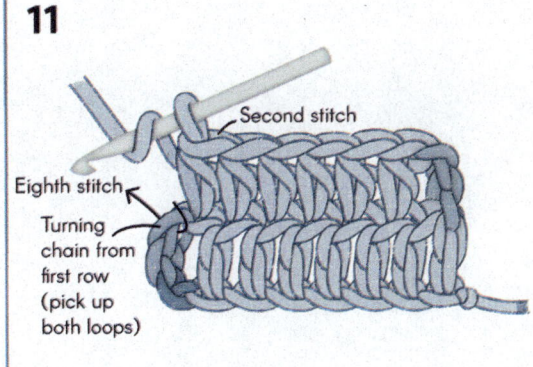

12 Make another turning chain upwards with two chains and rotate the piece to the other side.

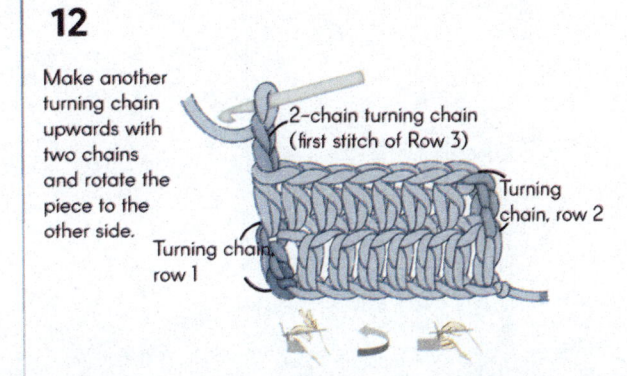

2-chain turning chain (first stitch of Row 3)
Turning chain, row 2
Turning chain, row 1

47

13 Make the other stitches on row 3 by following the same pattern.

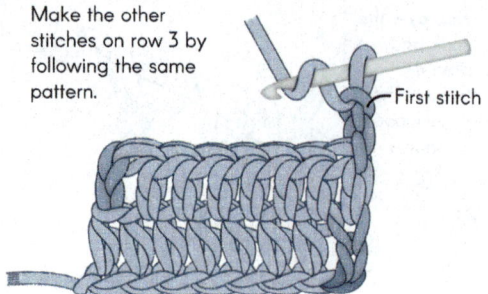

First stitch

14 Once you reach the eighth chain, make another turning chain.

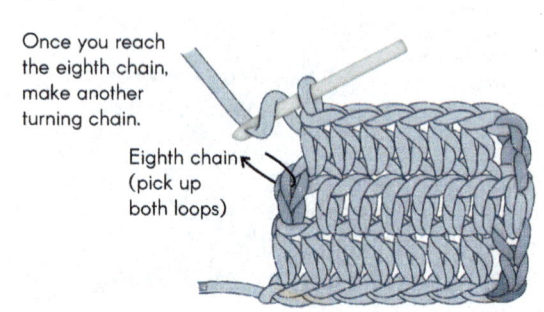

Eighth chain (pick up both loops)

15 Your half double crochet project should be completed by now.

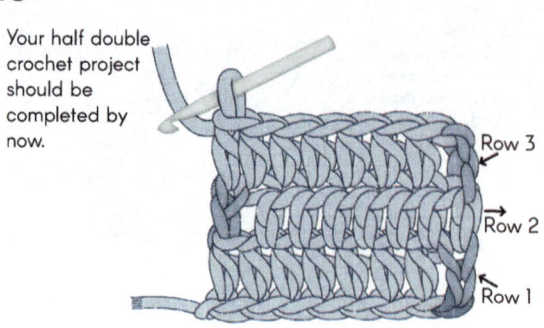

Row 3
Row 2
Row 1

2.6 The Treble Crochet Stitch

In treble or triple crochet, you make four chains from the foundation chain to make a turning chain. It is collectively called a stitch. It is twice as tall as the double crochet stitch. It is the kind of stitch best used for airy and textured projects meant to be draped over, such as shawls, scarves, etc.

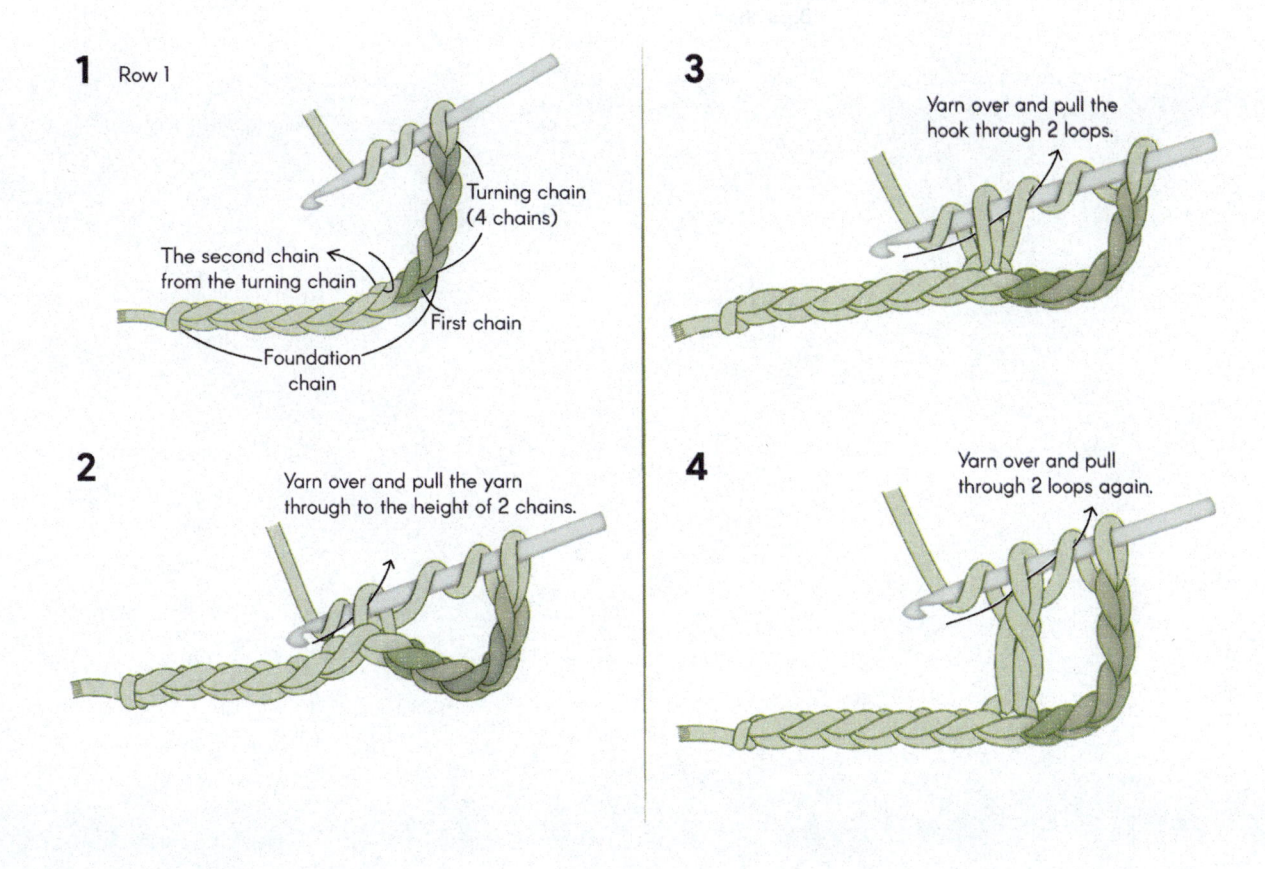

1 Row 1

Turning chain (4 chains)
The second chain from the turning chain
First chain
Foundation chain

2 Yarn over and pull the yarn through to the height of 2 chains.

3 Yarn over and pull the hook through 2 loops.

4 Yarn over and pull through 2 loops again.

5 Yarn over and pull through the last two loops.

6 Once the second stitch has four chains, move on to making others until you reach the end of the row.

Second stitch
First stitch
Turning chain
Base chain

7

First stitch

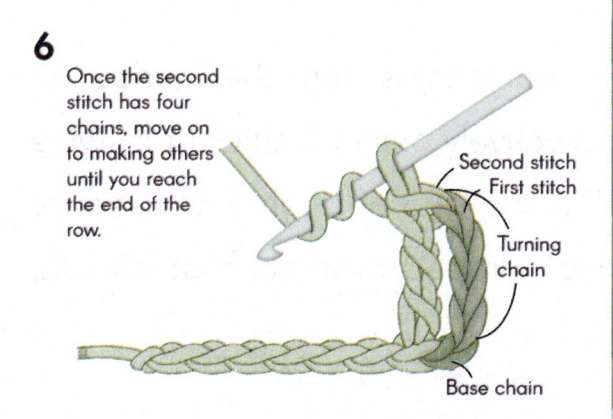

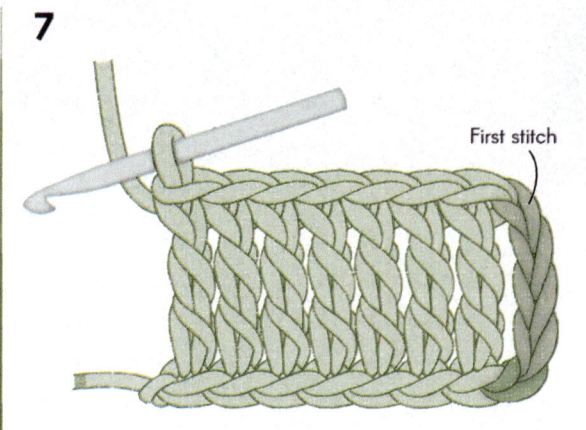

The first row is complete now. After working on the second row, the pattern should become more apparent.

2.7 Double Treble Crochet

Even taller than the treble crochet stitch, a double treble crochet needs five chains to make a turning chain. It needs to yarn over the hook thrice and be pulled through the two loops four times. It is best for open works.

1 Row 1

Make a foundation chain and a 5-chain turning chain at one end. Yarn over the hook three times before the next step.

Turning chain (3 chains)
Second chain
Base chain
Foundation chain

2

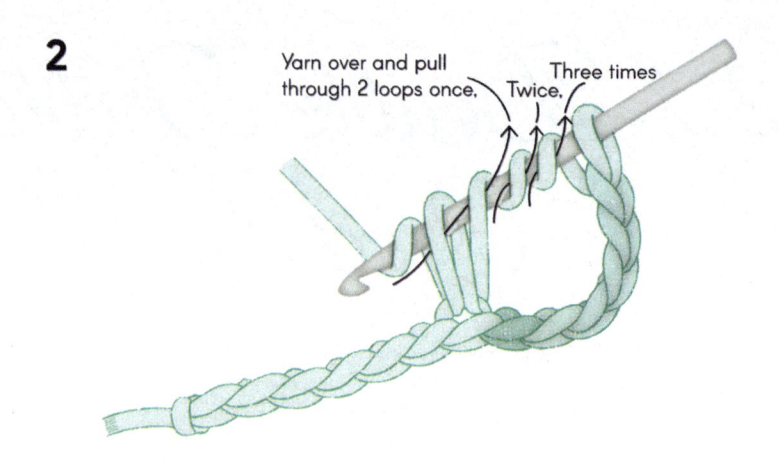

Yarn over and pull through 2 loops once. Twice. Three times.

3

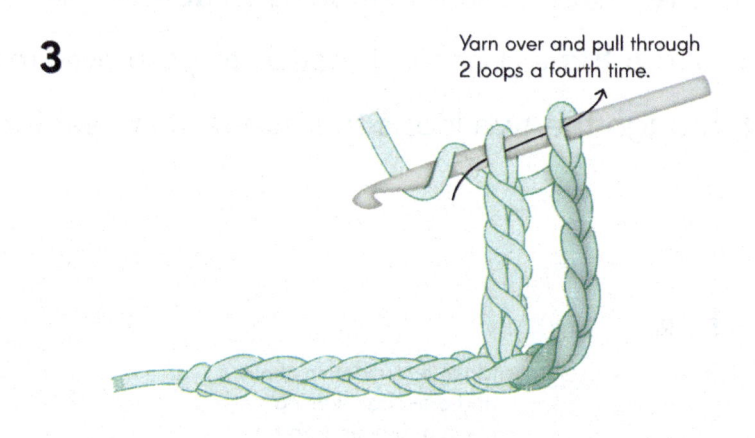

Yarn over and pull through 2 loops a fourth time.

4

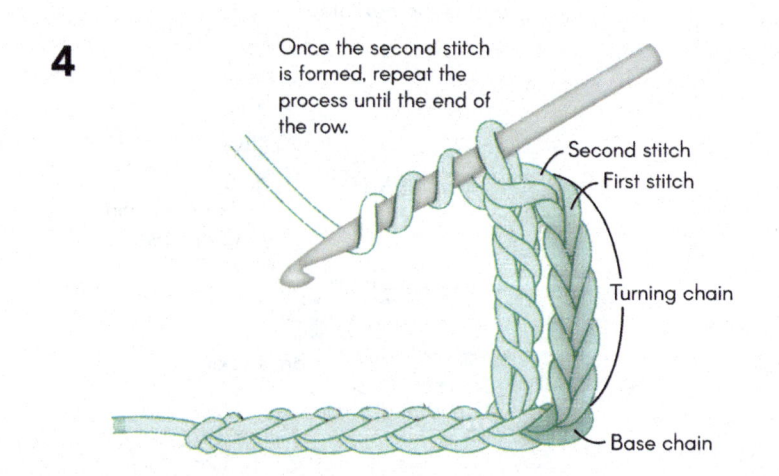

Once the second stitch is formed, repeat the process until the end of the row.

Second stitch
First stitch
Turning chain
Base chain

2.8 The Slip Stitch

Slip stitch is not usually used to make crochet but for other reasons, such as creating shapes and joining rounds. It certainly does not mean it cannot be used to make whole projects.

It is the most versatile stitch you will find in the basic stitches that every beginner must practice till perfection.

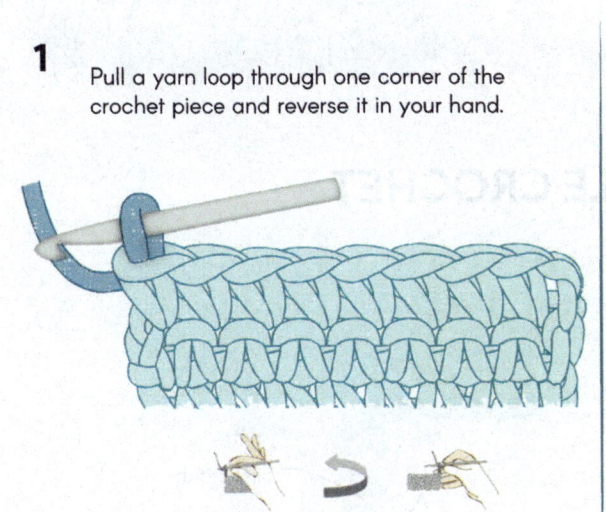

1 Pull a yarn loop through one corner of the crochet piece and reverse it in your hand.

2 Place the yarn on the side away from you, and insert the hook into the first stitch of the previous row.

First stitch

3 Yarn over and pull the yarn through the loop on the hook.

4 Once the first slip stitch is made, repeat the same process until you reach the end of the row.

First slip stitch

5 Tie the last stitch in the same way.

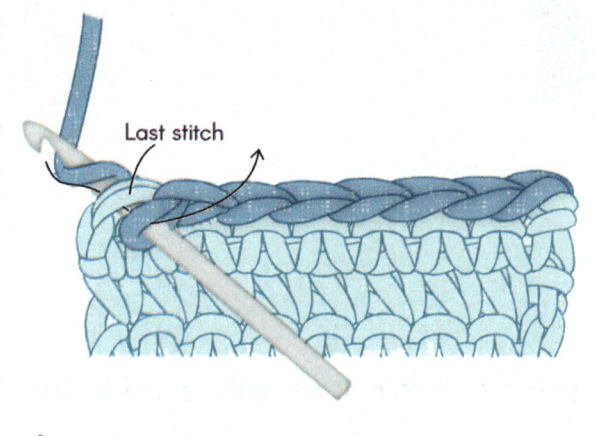

Last stitch

6 This is how it should look once your slip stitch is completed on a single crochet stitching piece.

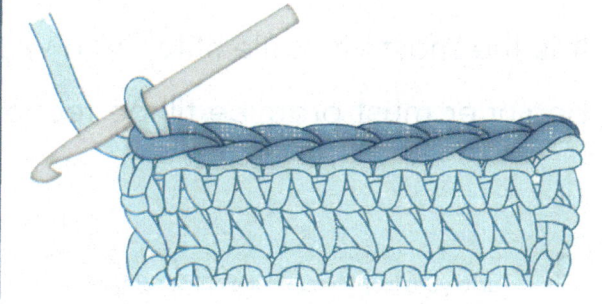

WITH DOUBLE CROCHET

1 Pick two loops from the corner stitch of the previous row. Make a loop onto the hook before passing it through. Pass it again from the second loop, as shown with the arrow.

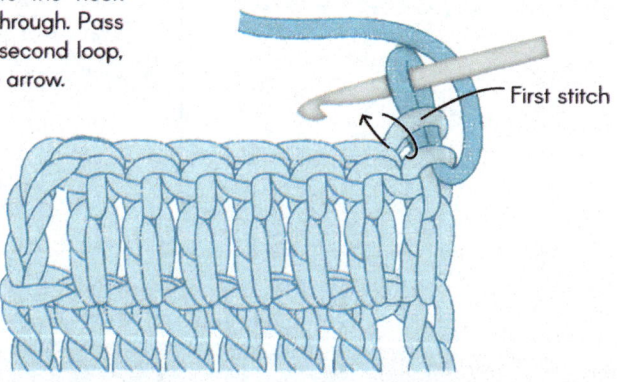

First stitch

2

The first slip stitch should look like this.

3

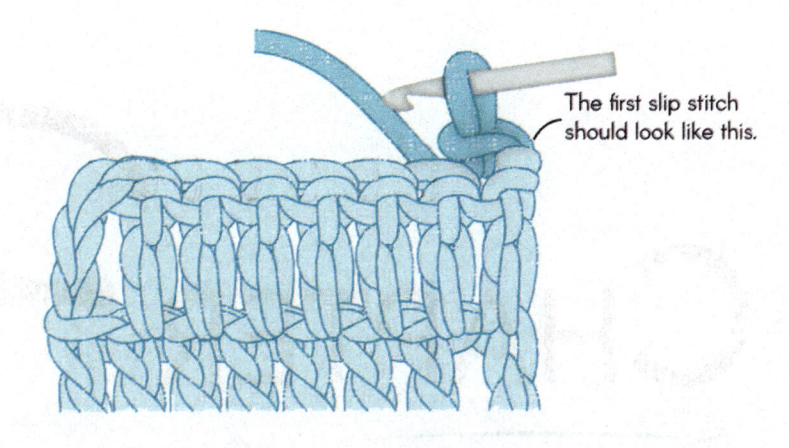

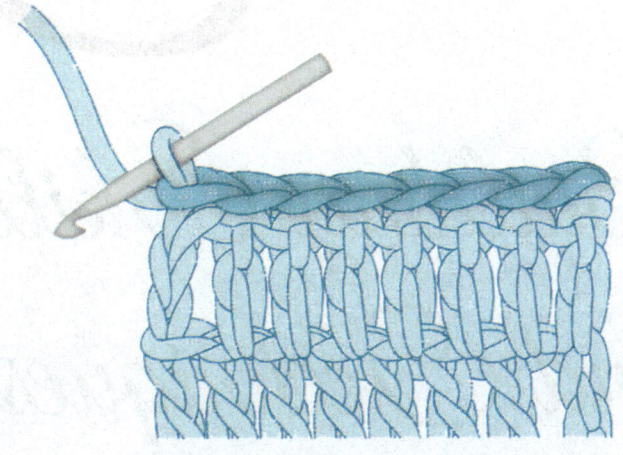

Follow the same pattern to make the whole row of slip stitches.

Chapter 3

Building Skills and Techniques

The basics are important, no matter what we do. But at the same time, we need to build relevant skill sets to adapt to any field we choose to enter. In crocheting, you need to go over the techniques mentioned in this chapter to know how it all comes together.

They will teach and interest you more to not only learn the tips and tricks to fix your mistakes but also to make your works more colorful and properly shaped for use.

3.1 Adjusting Stitches in the Foundation Chain

If, by any chance, the numbers of stitches were miscounted before and you need to rectify them, unravel the excess stitches by doing the following steps:

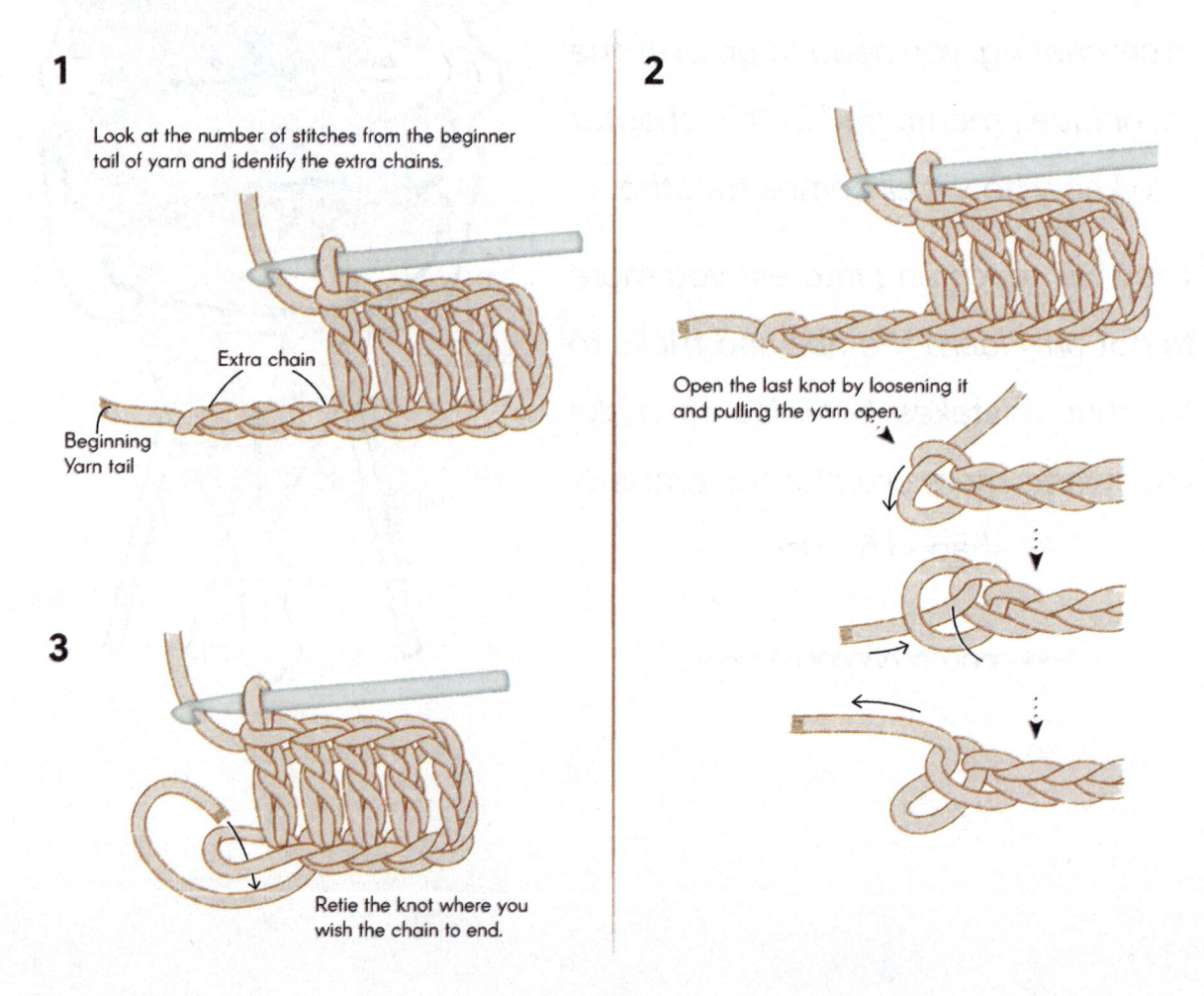

1

Look at the number of stitches from the beginner tail of yarn and identify the extra chains.

Extra chain

Beginning Yarn tail

2

Open the last knot by loosening it and pulling the yarn open.

3

Retie the knot where you wish the chain to end.

3.2 Increasing and Decreasing Stitches

Increasing and decreasing stitches are very useful in many situations if you want to add or subtract stitches from rows after a mistake or make elegant designs in your projects that require curving or making unusual shapes.

To Increase Stitches

When making an increase in a stitch, you put two or more stitches through the same stitch of the previous row. In picture 1, you can see a double crochet stitch into the stitch from the previous row. In the second picture, the same type of double stitch is repeated into the same stitch.

This method is called an increase in crocheting terms. This same pattern can be used for all other types of stitches. Increases can be made at any point of the row, according to your need. Usually, they make the crochet piece wider if you put them in the beginning or end. Similarly, they make crochet pieces bow up or out if the increase is anywhere in the middle part.

To Decrease Stitches

Decreasing stitches means that you are working on two or more stitches together at the same time. As opposed to an increased stitch, you make a stitch into a chain and make another to pull through together from the top, fashioning two stitches into one.

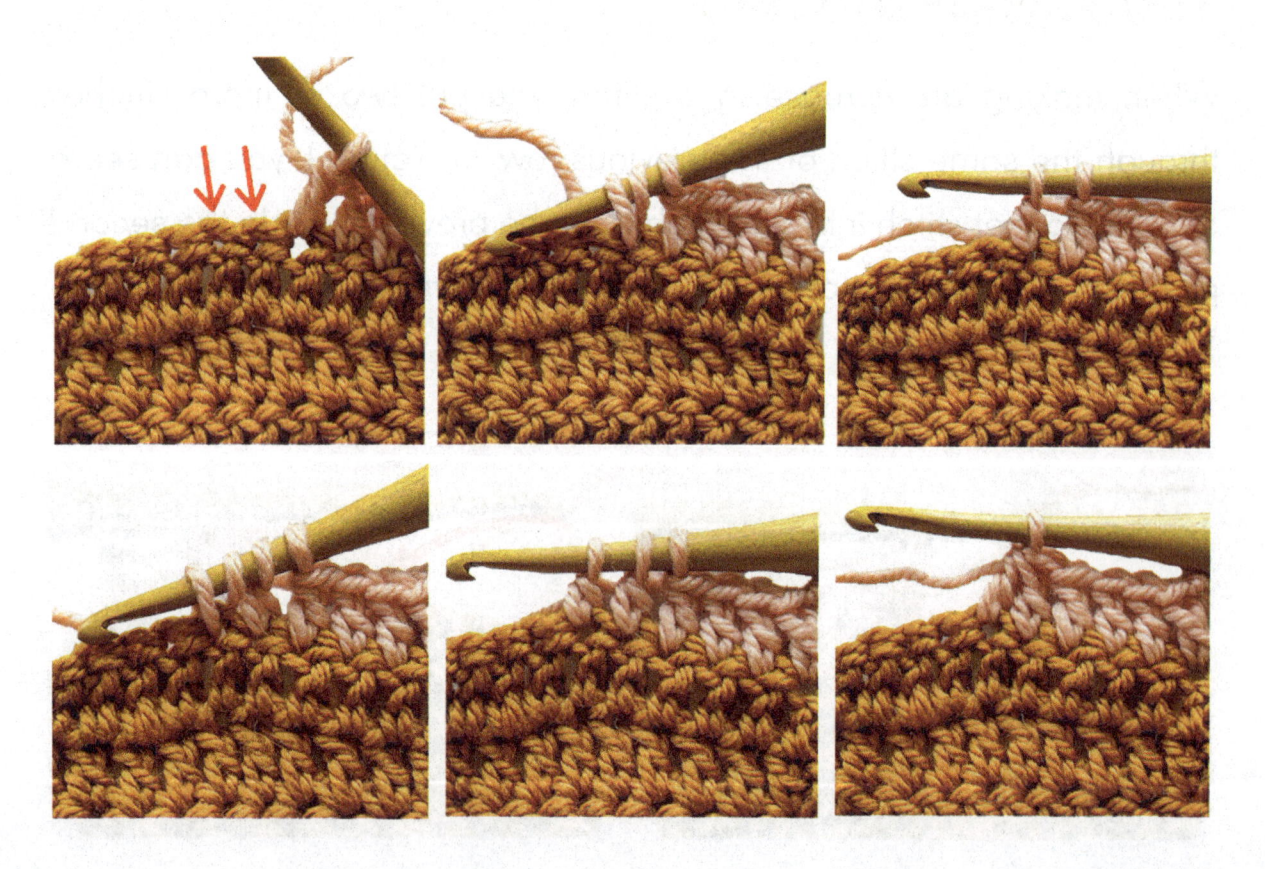

A decrease in a single crochet stitch is called a sc2tog, while a double crochet stitch is called a dc2tog. In dc2tog, first identify the stitches you need to decrease. Then, pull a loop through the first stitch and make a double crochet stitch there. Next, pull the yarn through the second stitch to make the second double crochet stitch.

The hook should have three loops of the yarn at this point. Yarn over and pull through to make a decrease.

3.3 Changing Yarn Colors

Changing yarn colors is a necessary skill to learn and practice in the early stages. It will help you make any item with various colors in play. I have used single crochet stitches in the instructions here, but you may use the same technique with any other basic stitch.

DIRECTIONS:

1. When you have created a row of stitches in one color and need to incorporate the new color from the next row, do the last yarn over of the row with the new color.

2. You should have two loops on the hook of color 1, as shown in the picture.

3. Now, place the color 2 on the hook as shown in the picture and make a slip knot to continue crocheting.

4. Now, pull the color 2 through the color 1 loops. Turn the piece of work in your hand and chain 1.

5. Make single stitches along the row (chain and make stitches according to the project; we have simply used single crochet stitches here). Your end result should look like this:

3.4 Weaving the Ends

In terms of weaving the ends after finishing a project, you have two options. Either use a hook or a yarn needle to weave. I do not recommend hooks, especially for beginners, because they can be difficult to maneuver. Nonetheless, they can be used.

On the other hand, yarn needles are smaller and easy to use. Simply thread the leftover yarn of the project into the yarn needle and make whipstitches (which will be explained later) or a knot through a few stitches to finish the weaving. However, beware that knots can make smooth pieces of work bumpy, so it is best to use whipstitches.

3.5 Making Gauge Swatch

Gauge swatch may sound like a lot of work, but it is the best way of making sure that your project is going smoothly before making too much progress that negatively impacts it.

Here is how you can make a gauge swatch:

- Once you have crocheted a piece that exceeds the 4"x 4" or 5"x 5" size, take a ruler and measure out the gauge size. Put pins at the corners to make sure the size is noted accurately.
- Count the number of stitches in a row that are within the pins. For instance, there are 7 ½ stitches in a 4"x 4" gauge.
- Next, count the number of rows present in that same area. For instance, there are four rows in that same 4"x 4" gauge.
- Now, you will make a calculation saying 4" gauge = 7 ½ stitches and four rows.
- By looking at the measurements provided by the pattern, you can assess if your stitches are tighter, looser, or just the same as provided by the others.

3.6 Using Blocking Technique

Blocking is a method that is used in crochet to straighten out the work project after or mid-completion. There are three ways you can use blocking to your advantage. These include:

Board Blocking

The most common method used in crochet is to apply water to the piece of work and put it on a blocking board by attaching pins to help it stay in shape. But not everyone has a blocking board available at home. You can easily straighten your work by using an iron board or an old couch seat to pin the work. But, it may not work for bigger projects that need bigger space.

Water Plunging and Towel Dry

Another method is to put your work into water till it is soaking wet. Pull it out and lay it on a big towel that can encompass it easily. Then, gently roll the towel to absorb the excess water and dry it by keeping it in proper shape.

Do not scrounge or wring it at any cost. It will destroy the shape of the piece again.

STEAM IRON

Using a steam iron is the easiest and quickest technique out of all three. Simply iron the piece until it has formed the taut shape required.

Chapter 4

12 Easy Crochet Projects

Crochet is one of the skills that you can use in your daily life with ease. Once you are familiar with the basics, use the projects to keep experimenting with the different stitches and items you can create from them. Better practice and eventual understanding can lead you to create a relaxing environment for your future self to enjoy thoroughly.

You can use the crocheted items for your own use or gift them to your close loved ones. This chapter will teach you 12 easy crochet projects that will provide you with plenty of practice and useful items to use in your daily life. Start with small and easy projects and move on to some bigger ones.

4.1 Granny Square

The granny square is the easiest and most basic project that most beginners make for better practice and to understand the workings of stitches joining together. Follow the instructions to make your own granny square.

MATERIALS NEEDED:

- Yarn (1 or 2 colors)
- Corresponding Hook (Size G-6 was used here)
- Scissors

DIRECTIONS:

The granny square is made by working the round shape. You don't need to turn your square to move on to the next round.

1. Make a chain of 4 stitches; join the first chain with the last through a slip stitch.

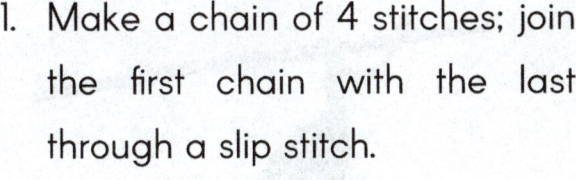

2. **Round 1:** chain 5 as a turning chain.

> **NOTE**
> If you have a one-color yarn, do not fasten it off. Instead, add a slip stitch to the corner space to finish up. But if you have two colors of yarn for the granny square, join them with a slip stitch in any 2 chain corner of each row.

3. Make 3 double crochet stitches around the ring shape.

4. Chain 3, as shown in the image.

5. Repeat step 3 by making three more double crochet stitches and making another chain of 3.

6. Repeat the same process to make the third panel by following the same procedure..

7. Make the last 3 chains of this round and insert the hook into the first stitch. Make a slip stitch to connect the ring.

8. **Round 2:** Make another chain of 5 to make another ring for the next round.

9. Make 3 double crochet stitches.

10. Chain 1 and add 3 double crochet stitches.

11. Repeat the step 10 again until the end, and secure the square with a slip stitch.

12. **Round 3:** Add the same or another color to make the third round. Follow the previous steps to make this round.

13. After completion, it should look like this:

Adding Rounds

You can grow your granny square as much as you want. Simply follow the same pattern of making rounds until you think the size is according to your needs.

4.2 Dishcloth

A dishcloth is an essential item in any household kitchen. It is an easy thing to make that simply requires concentration and attention to detail. Let's get into how you can crochet a dishcloth at home.

Materials Needed:

- 100% Cotton Yarn
- Corresponding Hook (size H-8 is used here)
- Scissors

> **Note**
> Dishcloths need to have tightly wounded stitches. Use the same size as I did, or make it more or less tight by using yarn and hook accordingly.

Directions:

1. Make chain stitches after tying a slipknot on the hook. Make 25 stitches in the row (it could be more according to the size you would like to make).
2. Once your row is complete, add another chain stitch (26, in my case). Consider this a turning chain, and pull your hook from the top of the second chain (going in the opposite direction you came from). Yarn over the hook.

3. Now, grab the hook and pull it from the three loops that are on the hook. Do not pull it too tightly because it will create unneeded tension in the dishcloth row.
4. Start making half-double crochet stitches until the end of row 2.
5. Repeat the same process for as many rows as you would like to make.
6. You can also add a border at the corners by making a single crochet row on all sides. At corners, you will need 2 or 3 stitches according to the size of the dishcloth.

WITHOUT BORDERS   **WITH BORDERS**

4.3 Easy Scarf

Scarfs are easy for beginners because the patterns are simple and easy for anyone to try. You don't have to study the instructions too hard or keep fretting over the length and width too much.

Once you get the hang of it, the possibilities of using scarves in your daily life are endless.

Materials Needed:

- Worsted Yarn
- Corresponding Hook (size K-10.5 is used here)
- Stitch Markers
- Yarn Needle
- Scissors

> **Note**
> Use stitch markers in your scarf to keep the count of the stitches. Put them after every 10 or 15 stitches to avoid losing the count.

Directions:

1. Start making the scarf by making a slipknot on the K hook. Leave about 5-6 inches of yarn on one side before making the knot.
2. Make 230 chain stitches for a length of about seven and a half feet (90 inches). You may add or subtract stitches according to the length you need. Do not count the loop you are working on; always count the stitches made before it.
3. Once the foundation chain is complete, start making single crochet stitches from the second chain from the hook. Make 230 single stitches along the row.
4. Make a chain stitch at the end of this row to use as a turning chain. Flip the piece horizontally to work from the opposite side.
5. On top of your single stitches row, you will find two loops. Make another row of single stitches using those two loops from the previous row. Complete the row with another turning chain and move on to the next row.

6. Make as many rows of the scarf as you like while keeping the number of stitches in mind. You can ruin the shape by adding or subtracting a stitch from the required number. So, make sure the stitches are in order.
7. In the last row, do not make a turning chain in the end. Leave the same amount of yarn you left at the beginning of the scarf. Loop the yarn around your hook and pull it through the last active loop of the scarf that was already looped to the hook.
8. Tug it gently afterward to ensure it is tight. Use a yarn needle to weave both of the ends into the scarf.

4.4 Beanie

Beanies are a must for cold winter days. If you are looking to make a beanie to go along with your scarf, this is the most fun way to spend your time.

The beanie you see here has been made to be about 6 inches in length and 7 inches in width at the bottom. You can also customize the size according to your needs, but I recommend the given size for first-timers to set their hand on them.

Materials Needed:

- Light Worsted Cotton Yarn
- Corresponding Hook (size H-8 is used here)
- Yarn Needle
- Scissors

Directions:

For Round 1:

1. Start making a magic circle by making a loose knot. Chain 2 on it, as shown in the picture. Do not count it as a stitch.
2. Make 12 double crochet stitches in a circle. Pull the yarn from the non-working end of the previous loose knot to close the circle.
3. Make a slip stitch on the top of the first stitch of the round 1.

For Round 2:

4. Make a chain of 2.

5. Use 2 double crochet stitches in each stitch and make a complete round on the same pattern.

6. Make a slip stitch on top of the first stitch of the round.

For Round 3:

7. Make a chain of 2 and add a double stitch into the same stitch.
8. In the next stitch, make 2 double crochet stitches into the same stitch.
9. As explained before, follow the pattern of 1 double stitch, then 2 double stitches to complete the round.
10. Make a slip stitch on the first stitch of the row when the circle is complete.

For Round 4:

11. Make another chain of 2.
12. Do 1 double crochet stitch in each of the next two stitches.
13. Make 2 double crochet stitches in one stitch.
14. Follow the pattern of 1 double crochet stitch in 2 stitches and then 2 double crochet stitches in one stitch till the round is complete.
15. Make a slip stitch on top of the first stitch of the round.

For Round 5:

16. For the first stitch, make 1 single crochet and 2 double crochet stitches in the same stitch.
17. Skip the next two stitches.
18. Follow this same pattern of making 1 single and 2 double crochet stitches in the same stitch and then skipping two stitches to make another stitch on the same pattern.
19. Make a slip stitch on top of the first single stitch.

For Round 6:

20. Pick the first single crochet and make 1 single and 2 double crochet stitches within one stitch.

> Only make the stitches of this round in the loops of single crochet stitches from the previous round.

21. Follow the same pattern until the end of the round.
22. Make a slip stitch on top of the first single crochet stitch.

ROUND 7 (AND ONWARDS):

23. Follow the round six instructions for this and any more rounds till you reach your desired length.
24. Weave off the end of the yarn with the yarn needle after looping about 4-6 inches of yarn on the hook and pulling through.

4.5 Simple Baby Blanket

Blankets are a necessary item when kids are involved. It is one of the simplest techniques to use in crochet practice. Moreover, if you don't have kids at home, you can always make it to give it away. It will add a personalized touch to your gifts. Or, you can make a bigger blanket with this technique to use it yourself.

My blanket is in three colors, but at first, you can try to use one color for ease. If you need more than one color, divide the number of rows for each color and keep changing the colors accordingly.

MATERIALS NEEDED:

- Yarn about 6 skeins in one color (varies according to the size)
- Corresponding Hook (hooks H-8 and J-10 were used here)
- Yarn Needle
- Scissors

DIRECTIONS:

1. With a J-10 hook, make a foundation chain of about 150 stitches. You can make less or more stitches according to your desired width.
2. Switch to the H-8 hook. From the 2nd chain, make a slip stitch and add a half double crochet stitch in the next stitch.
3. Use half double crochet stitches in the entire row and make a slip stitch in place of the last stitch.
4. Chain 1 and turn the work to make another row of half double crochet stitches from the other side.
5. Repeat the same process to crochet the entire blanket while counting the rows (I made 125 rows for mine).
6. You can use different colored yarns like I have or just one according to your need or ease. The finished product should be around 32 inches x 28 inches.
7. Use a yarn needle to weave the ends.

4.6 Hot Pad

Hot pads may not sound much interesting, but they are very much needed in a household. Most of the cooking pans cannot be placed randomly. Use these hot pads to make space on the stove and kitchen when faced with limitations.

You can use any color of yarn that goes well with your kitchen and home settings.

MATERIALS NEEDED:

- Cotton Yarn (Medium-4)
- Corresponding Hook (hook H-8 was used here)
- Yarn Needle
- Scissors

DIRECTIONS:

1. Make a magic ring as you made in making a beanie. Use 12 double crochet stitches to make the ring and tighten the middle ring by pulling the beginning piece of thread that is not being worked.
2. Make a slip stitch on the top of the first stitch.
3. For 2nd round, make a chain of 2, and add 2 double stitches in the 2 chain space.
4. Make 2 double stitches in a single stitch space for the whole round.
5. Make a slip stitch at the top of the first double crochet stitch.
6. In the third round, chain 2 and add a double crochet stitch in the same chain space.
7. Make 2 double crochet stitches in the next stitch, then do 1 double crochet stitch in the next stitch, and 2 double crochet stitches afterward. Repeat this same pattern till the end of the round.
8. Make another slip stitch to the top of the first double crochet of the round.
9. Follow the steps of the third round to make a total of seven rounds.
10. Weave in the ends after completion.

> ## TIP!
>
> You can also make a coaster set to match with the hot pads. Simply follow the steps up to step 8. Measure the coasters to work around the diameter of about 4 ½ inches. Similarly, hot pads should be 7 ½ inches in diameter.

4.7 Pillow Cover

Trendy pillow covers always stay in style. If you want to spruce up your place with new pillow covers to bring new vibrancy around your place, make these covers as soon as possible!

For that, you will need to make one front panel for the pillow cover and two back panels. One back panel will cover a bit of the other panel because it will need to come over to close the buttons at the back.

The only catch is you need to make this design in a back loop! But don't worry; it's just new for you, not difficult!

BACK LOOP IN SINGLE CROCHET STITCH

Make a row of any common stitch as foundation chain. Chain only the back loops for making the next row instead of taking both loops as done in basic stitches.

In a chain, loop towards you is front loop and the loop away from you is back loop.

MATERIALS NEEDED:

- 4 Skeins of Yarn (Super Bulky-6)
- Corresponding Hook (hook M/N-13 was used here)
- Yarn Needle
- Pillow Insert (18" by 18" used here, could be changed to any size)
- Buttons (3 used here)
- Matching Thread
- Sewing Needle
- Scissors

Directions:

The pillow has vertical lines, so the rows will be made vertically. Keep it in mind while making the panels.

Pillow Front Panel:

1. Make a foundation chain of 36 stitches. From the second chain from the hook, make single stitches across the row.

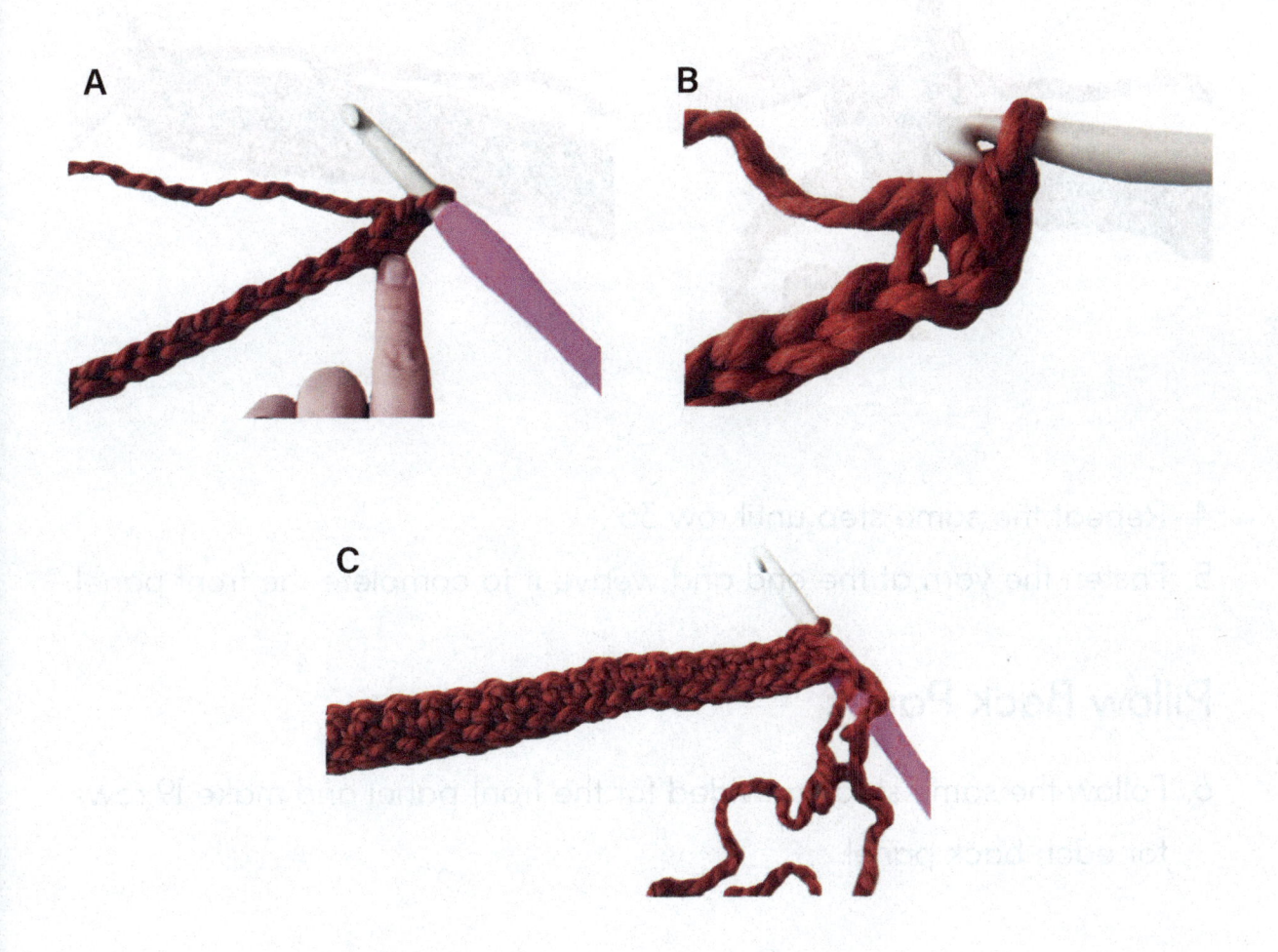

A

B

C

2. After making the chain of 35 stitches, turn the piece of work.
3. From the 2nd row onwards, chain 1. Make single stitches in the back loop for the whole row, and then turn the piece to work on another row.

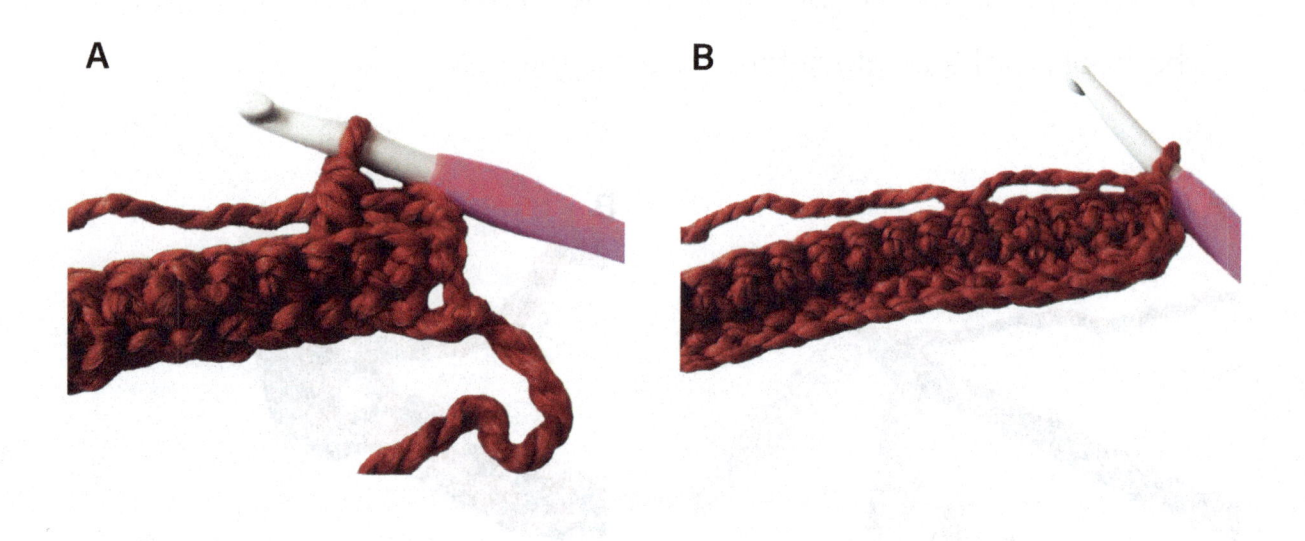

A

B

4. Repeat the same step until row 36.
5. Fasten the yarn at the end and weave it to complete the front panel.

Pillow Back Panel:

6. Follow the same steps provided for the front panel and make 19 rows for each back panel.

Sewing the Panels Together:

7. Sew the back left-side panel to the front by sewing along the three outer edges.

8. Sew the right-side panel as shown here. It will overlap on the left panel, which is precisely how we want it.

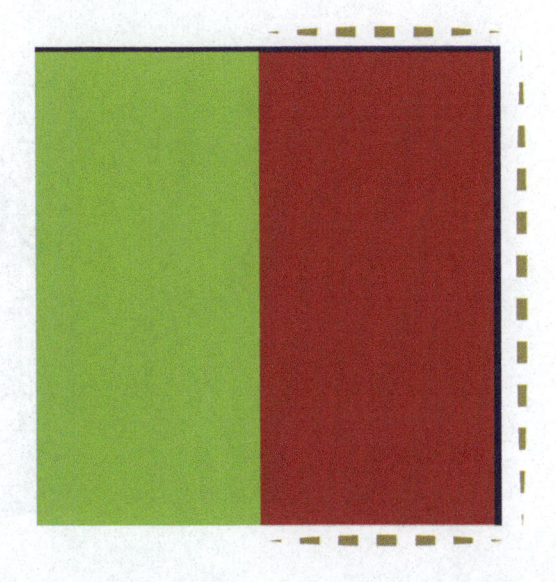

9. Sew the buttons along the left panel first and overlap the other panel to see the best spot for the buttons to get through.

10. Pull the buttons from a stitch before them to close the back panels. With that, your pillow cover is ready.

4.8 Laptop Case

Laptops are essential for many reasons these days. It is best to keep them protected by using hand-made cases. Make your own laptop cover case by following the instructions given ahead!

Materials Needed:

- 2 Balls of Acrylic Yarn (Super-Bulky-6)
- Corresponding Hook (size N was used here)
- 1 Button (medium or large size)
- Yarn Needle
- Scissors

Directions:

1. Make a chain of 21 stitches in the foundation row.
2. In row 1, make out the second chain from the hook's placement and make 20 single stitches in the row.
3. Repeat the same step from rows 2 to 35.
4. In the last row, follow the same pattern to make ten stitches, then make a chain of 3, skip a stitch, and then keep on making single stitches along the row.
5. Weave in the ends.

Binding the Cover:

6. Lay down the piece on a flat space, such as a table, and fold the piece. Leave around 4 rows of above stitches to be folded over for the flap.
7. Now, take the yarn needle and make whipstitches along the sides to bind it together.

WHIPSTITCH LOOKS LIKE THIS!

Simply make a stitch that connects two pieces together and pass the needle from the corner stitches to bind both sides.

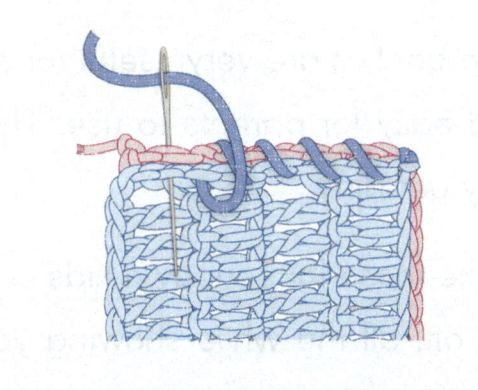

8. Weave the ends before sewing the button on the front panel.
9. Make sure it is directly proportional to the buttonhole left before.

OPTIONAL!

You can also block your cover by ironing it lightly first (because of acrylic yarn). It should straighten out your laptop cover and give it proper shape.

4.9 Yarn Booties for Kids

Yarn booties are very useful for smaller kids. They are soft, comfortable, and easy for parents to use. They can wash and reuse these easily if they get dirty.

Make these for your own kids or use them as another incredible item to gift off, all the while showing your care, support, and love to the little ones.

Materials Needed:

- Hook (size 7 for 9-12 months old baby, smaller for less age bracket)
- Yarn (Light Worsted-3)
- Yarn Needle
- Scissors

Directions:

For Making Sole:

1. Make a foundation chain of 13 chain stitches.
2. In round 1, make a double crochet stitch in the 4th chain from the hook (skip the 3 chains and don't count it as a stitch.
3. Make 1 double crochet stitch in the next 8 chains. In that last chain, make 8 double crochet stitches in the same stitch. It should make a semi-circle shape of the row.
4. Make 1 double crochet stitch in the next 8 chains. Make 7 double crochet stitches in the last chain and make a slip stitch to join it with the 1st stitch.
5. For round 2, make a chain of 3 (not a stitch). Make 2 double crochet stitches in that same stitch.
6. Use 1 double crochet stitch in the 8 stitches and use 2 double crochet stitches in the next 8 stitches around the semi-circle.
7. Make 1 double crochet stitch for the next 8 stitches and 2 double crochet stitches in 7 remaining stitches. Make a slip stitch to join it to the 1st stitch of the round.

For Making Mid-Section:

8. For round 3, make a chain of 3 and make a back loop double crochet stitch in the same stitch.
9. Repeat the back loop double crochet stitches for the next 47 stitches. Make a slip stitch at the end to join it to the 1st stitch of the round.

For Shaping the Toe:

10. In round 4, chain 1 and make a single crochet stitch in the same stitch. Make single crochet stitches for the next 9 stitches.
11. Double crochet 2 stitches together (in each stitch, abbreviated as dc2tog) 8 times before making 22 single crochet stitches. After the last stitch, make a slip stitch to join it to the 1st stitch of the round.
12. In round 5, chain 1 and make a single crochet stitch in the same stitch. Make 9 single crochet stitches and dc2tog 4 times.
13. Make 22 single crochet stitches and then a slip stitch.
14. For round 6, follow the same pattern as round 5, but dc2tog only twice, and for round 7, only once. The rest is all the same.

For Making the Upper Section:

15. In round 8, chain 1 and make a single crochet stitch in that same stitch. Make 32 single crochet stitches and make a slip stitch to join the last stitch with the first one of the round.
16. Repeat the same process of round 8 for the next rounds (from round 9 to 17).
17. Once done, cut the yarn and weave the ends.
18. Fold the booties from above to create a cuff.

4.10 Small-Sized Amigurumi Cat

Toys are a favorite for kids worldwide, but cute and small toys are especially popular with many young teens and adults too. Make these small yarn toys for any reason you want. Be it for yourself, others, or for decorative purposes.

It is the most accessible type of accessory you can make with just a skein of yarn and a hook. You can also make it a keychain (if it is smaller in size). The possibilities are endless!

Materials Needed:

- Yarn (1 or 2 colors, according to need)
- Corresponding Hook (size C-2 was used here)
- Yarn Needle
- Stuffing
- Pink and Black colored threads (to add details such as eyes and ears)
- Sewing Needle
- Scissors

Directions:

Making Cat Body:

1. Make a magic ring of 6 single stitches in a row.
2. In round 2, make 2 single crochet stitches in each stitch.
3. In round 3, make a single crochet stitch and then 2 single crochet stitches in the next stitch. Repeat the same pattern around.
4. In round 4, make a single crochet stitch in the next 2 stitches, and then 2 single crochet stitches in one stitch (abbreviated as sc2tog). Repeat the same pattern around.
5. In round 5, make a single crochet stitch in the next 3 stitches, and then make a sc2tog in the next stitch. Repeat the same pattern around.
6. In round 6, make a single crochet stitch in the next 4 stitches, and

then make a sc2tog in the next stitch. Repeat the same pattern around.

7. In rounds 7 and 8, make single crochet stitches all around.
8. In round 9, make a single crochet stitch in the next 4 stitches, and then make a sc2tog in the next stitch. Repeat the same pattern around.
9. In rounds 10-12, make single crochet stitches all around.
10. In round 13, make a single crochet stitch in the next 3 stitches, and then make a sc2tog in the next stitch. Repeat the same pattern around.
11. In rounds 14-17, make single crochet stitches all around.
12. In round 18, make a single crochet stitch in the next 2 stitches, and then make a sc2tog in the next stitch. Repeat the same pattern around.
13. In round 19, make single crochet stitches all around.
14. Make the eyes and face of the cat by using black thread and a needle before stuffing the cat.
15. In round 20, pick both sides of the crocheted piece together to seal them off by crocheting them together.
16. Make a double crochet stitch in the first stitch. Make 7 single crochet stitches and make another double crochet stitch as the last stitch. Weave in the ends to finish making the body of the cat.

MAKING CAT TAIL:

17. Make a magic ring of 5 single crochet stitches in a row.
18. For round 2, make 2 single crochet stitches in each stitch.
19. In round 3, make single crochet stitches around the circle.
20. Make a sc2tog and make 3 single crochet stitches after it in round 4. Repeat the same step to complete the round.
21. In rounds 5-6, make single crochet stitches in the round.
22. Make a sc2tog and make 3 single crochet stitches after it in round 7. Repeat the same step to complete the round.
23. Stuff the tail by filling the end lightly.
24. In rounds 8-15, make single crochet stitches in the round.
25. Bind the tail by closing the ends. Take a yarn needle to attach the tail to the toy and weave it in the ends.

> ### NOTE
> You may use 2 colors in yarn to make the stripes in the cat. Change the color in every 2-3 rounds to give a uniform look.

4.11 Summer Top

Summer tops are very popular and trendy these days. You can easily make this at home, and the best news is that it's a free-size item that most people can use without having to take care of precise measurements that may or may not translate well later.

The top given here is 32 inches long. You can add or subtract rows according to your desired length.

Materials Needed:

- Yarn (Light-3)
- Corresponding Hook (size J-10 was used here)
- Yarn Needle
- Scissors
- Stitch Markers (optional)

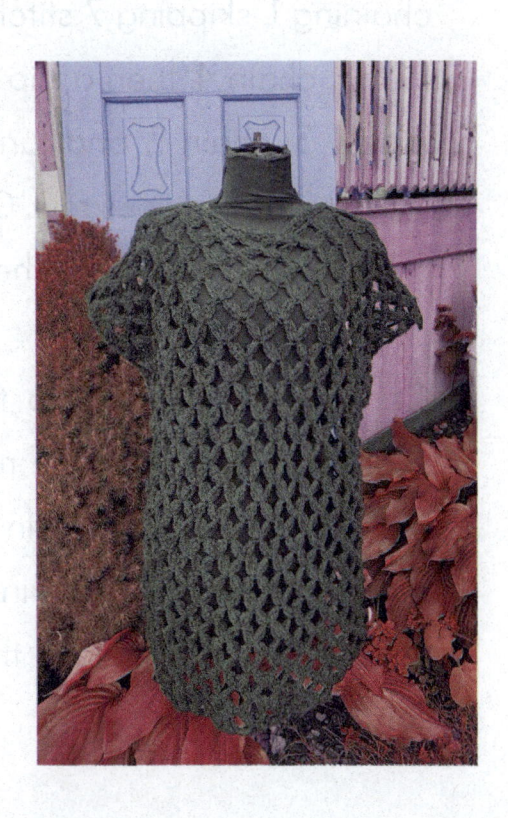

Directions:

Make two panels by following the given instructions.

1. Make a chain of 106 stitches.
2. For row 1, make the first single crochet stitch from the second chain from the hook. Make single crochet stitches along the whole row.
3. In row 2, chain 4, turn the piece in your hand. Make 2 treble crochet stitches together in the first stitch (abbreviated as tr2tog).
4. Chain 1 and skip 7 stitches to make tr2tog again. Chain 4 and make a slip stitch into that same stitch. Once again, chain 4 and make another tr2tog into the same stitch.
5. Follow the step 4 along the row till the end. Finish the row with chaining 1, skipping 7 stitches to get to the last stitch, which needs a tr2tog, chain 4, then a slip stitch into this same stitch.
6. In row 3, chain 7, and turn the piece. Make a tr2tog in the chain 1 stitch of the previous row. Chain 4 and make a slip stitch in that same chain 1 stitch. Make another chain of 4 and tr2tog again in that same stitch.
7. Chain 1 and move onto the next chain 1 stitch of the row by making tr2tog. Chain 4, make a slip stitch, chain 4 again, and tr2tog into that same stitch.

> ### Triple Treble Crochet Stitch
>
> It simply requires two more yarn overs than treble crochet stitch and one more yarn over than double treble crochet stitch.

8. Repeat the same process as step 7 across the rest of the row. Make a triple treble crochet stitch into the single crochet stitch of row 1.
9. In row 4, chain 4 and turn the piece. Make a tr2tog on top of the triple treble crochet stitch of the previous row.
10. Chain 1 and move onto the next chain 1 stitch of the row by making tr2tog. Chain 4, make a slip stitch, chain 4 again, and tr2tog into that same stitch.
11. Repeat the same process as step 10 across the row. Make a tr2tog, chain 4, and make a slip stitch on top of the chain 7 of the previous row.
12. In row 5, chain 7 and turn the project. Make a tr2tog in the chain 1 stitch of the previous row. Chain 4 and make a slip stitch in that same chain 1 stitch. Make another chain of 4 and tr2tog again in that same stitch.
13. Chain 1 and move onto the next chain 1 stitch of the row by making tr2tog. Chain 4, make a slip stitch, chain 4 again, and tr2tog into that same stitch.
14. Repeat the same process as step 13 across the rest of the row. Make a triple treble crochet stitch into the triple treble crochet stitch previously made in 2 rows above.
15. For rows 6-33, repeat the instructions for rows 4 and 5 till you reach the end. Use step 24 to make the end stitch for each row.
16. In row 34, make a chain of 1 and turn the top in your hand. Make a single crochet stitch on top of the triple treble crochet stitch.

17. Chain 7 and make a single crochet stitch into the chain 1 stitch. Repeat this same pattern till the end of the row. Finish the row by making a chain of 7 and making a single crochet stitch on chain 7 of the previous row.
18. In row 35, chain 1 and turn the piece. Make a single crochet stitch in the first stitch and repeat it until the end of the row.

JOINING THE PANELS:

19. Once both panels are done, place them together by placing their right sides facing each other. The first panel is placed with the right side up and the second with the right side down to join together.

> **RIGHT SIDE**
> The front of your work project is usually termed Right Side in Crochet.
>
> **WRONG SIDE**
> Subsequently, the back of your work project is named Wrong Side in Crochet.

20. Start sewing the wrong sides. First, sew the last 3 stitches of row 35 together on both ends.
21. Then, count the 4 petals from one end of both panels and sew through the single crochet stitch that comes after it on the same row (35). Tie a knot and cut the yarn. Repeat the same step on the other side.
22. Count the rows from there and skip 12 before joining the sides of the panels.
23. Weave in any ends left once the panels are attached

4.12 Loose Cardigan

Make a loose and baggy cardigan by using the technique taught here. It is an easy but lengthy process that will help beginners like you to get into the habit of making different parts of the same project and attaching them together.

It may seem like a difficult task, but it is simply more time-consuming than difficult to follow along. You can always use 2 or more colored yarns to make multi-colored cardigans for yourself and others.

Materials Needed:

- Yarn (Light-2) [5 yarn balls for S/M, 6 yarn balls for L/XL]
- Corresponding Hook (size G-6 was used here)
- Yarn Needle
- Scissors
- Stitch Markers (optional)

Directions:

Making Back Panel:

1. Start by making a foundation chain of 100.
2. In row 1, make a double crochet stitch in the third chain from the hook. Make double crochet stitches till the end of the row.
3. In row 2, chain 2 and turn the piece before making double crochet stitches along the row.
4. Repeat the step 3 for all rows ahead (till row 48 for small and medium size and row 52 for large and extra-large size)
5. Finish the panel work by weaving in the ends.

Making Front Panels:

Make 2 panels from the given instructions.

6. Make a chain of 50 chain stitches.
7. In row 1, double crochet in the third stitch from the hook. Make double crochet stitches along the row.
8. In row 2, make a chain of 2 and turn the panel. Make double crochet stitches in the whole row.
9. Follow the pattern of row 2 in the rest of the rows. Make 48 rows in total for S/M sizes and 52 rows for L/XL sizes.
10. Weave in the ends along the way.

Making Sleeves:

Make 2 sleeves from the given instructions.

11. Make 60 chain stitches for the foundation row.

12. In row 1, make double crochet stitches from the third chain from the hook till the end of the row.
13. In row 2, chain 2 and turn the sleeve. Make double crochet stitches in the whole row.
14. Repeat the step 13 for all rows ahead. Make 36 rows for S/M size and 37 for L/XL.
15. Once the rows are completed, leave a long tail at the end and make the seam later.

Assembling of the Cardigan:

16. Lay down the back panel on a flat surface. Arrange the front panels on top of it while leveling them perfectly.
17. Cut yarn by measuring it to be twice the length of a panel. Make seams to attach the panels with whipstitches. For S/M size, start seaming from below up to 33 rows. For L/XL size, start seaming from below up to 35 rows.
18. Now, seam both of the front panels to the back one by using another piece of yarn to whipstitch.

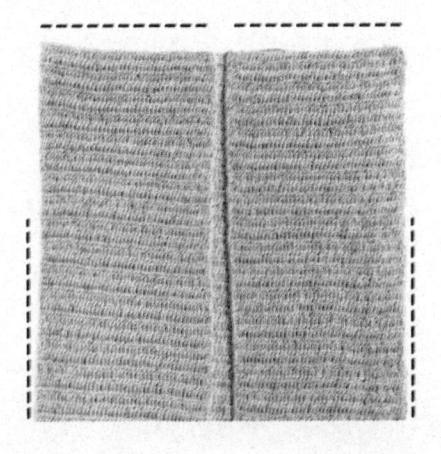

19. Next, sew the sleeves using the same method. Fold the sleeve and make whipstitches along the fold from the yarn that was left before. Prepare both sleeves to attach to the cardigan.

20. Now, turn your sleeveless cardigan (just for now sleeveless) inside out and pass on the sleeve you are going to attach from the inside of the cardigan. Align it perfectly with the sleeve opening to seam together.
21. Seam along the edges by being careful not to shut the sleeve holes accidentally. Use whipstitches to sew both sleeves as well.
22. End the work by weaving in any leftover yarn.

Conclusion

I have enjoyed making this book immensely, and I hope it has been fun for all the beginners in crochet. It may seem like a daunting and difficult hobby or task to take up when you are unaware of its working, and potential uses. The fact that you have reached here proves that at least you are willing to try. For that reason, I commend you!

Now, you may have noticed that I have been emphasizing the importance of practicing throughout the book. I did so because crocheting is one thing that only needs you to use your hands to get familiar with everything that has been taught here. The key to becoming an expert in crochet-making is to keep giving yourself new challenges. Master one thing and find another; that way, you are bound to make things that are not only useable but giftable or even sellable.

Just keep working on your flow, and everything else will start making sense to you. Another great motivator is to make things that you need (for yourself or the house). It will make you strive to improve your crocheting skills over time. And, of course, "Crochet for Beginners" will guide you along the way.

So, take care of yourself, and don't forget to post your projects in the comments section to show off your newly acquired skills! I will be eagerly waiting!

About the Author

Leta Murphy is a crochet hobbyist who has recently started to impart her extensive crochet knowledge to others after 21 years of practice. She first started sewing at the age of 14. Later, she decided to expand her horizons by learning knitting and crochet. Although she can sew and knit, crochet has been her go-to activity since the day she understood how it all worked.

She has now started teaching some people interested in crocheting in her social circle. She hopes to open her own classes where not only crocheting but also knitting and sewing can be taught to people of all ages.

Made in the USA
Columbia, SC
27 February 2025